SpringerBriefs in Economics

For further volumes:
http://www.springer.com/series/8876

Kristof Van Assche · Raoul Beunen
Martijn Duineveld

Evolutionary Governance Theory

An Introduction

Springer

Kristof Van Assche
Strategic Communication
Wageningen University
Wageningen
The Netherlands

Martijn Duineveld
Cultural Geography
Wageningen University
Wageningen
The Netherlands

Raoul Beunen
Strategic Communication
Wageningen University
Wageningen
The Netherlands

ISSN 2191-5504 ISSN 2191-5512 (electronic)
ISBN 978-3-319-00983-4 ISBN 978-3-319-00984-1 (eBook)
DOI 10.1007/978-3-319-00984-1
Springer Cham Heidelberg New York Dordrecht London

Library of Congress Control Number: 2013942655

Printed on acid-free paper

Springer is part of Springer Science+Business Media (www.springer.com)

Investigations that are inspired theoretically can always be accused of a lack of 'practical reference'. They do not provide prescriptions for others to use. They observe practice and occasionally ask what is to be gained by making such a hasty use of incomplete ideas. This does not exclude the possibility that serviceable results can be attained in this way. But then the significance of the theory will always remain that a more controlled method of creating ideas can increase the probability of more serviceable results - above all, that it can reduce the probability of creating useless excitement.

Luhmann 1989

We must walk on the razor's edge, eschewing the extremes of representationalism (objectivism) and solipsism (idealism).

Maturana and Varela 1987

Ch-ch-ch-ch-changes. Turn and face the strange.

David Bowie 1971

Preface

Evolutionary Governance Theory: An Introduction, offers the reader a remarkable new perspective on the way markets, institutions and societies evolve together. It can be of use to anyone interested in market and public sector reform, development, public administration, politics and law. Based on a wide variety of case studies on three continents and a variety of conceptual sources, the authors develop a theory that clarifies the nature and functioning of dependencies that mark governance evolutions. This in turn delineates in an entirely new manner the spaces open for policy experiment. As such, it offers a new mapping of the middle ground between libertarianism and social engineering. Theoretically, the approach draws on a wide array of sources: institutional and development economics, systems theories, post-structuralism, actor-network theories, discourse theory, planning theory and legal studies.

Wageningen

Kristof Van Assche
Raoul Beunen
Martijn Duineveld

Contents

Part I
Introduction

Chapter 1
Introduction

Understanding change has become one of the most important challenges for contemporary governance and its theories. The global economic crisis has shown that researchers and practitioners in many different fields and disciplines face great difficulties in understanding and explaining unexpected events and changes in our society. An insufficient grasp of the different mechanisms that drive the evolution of governance, a partial and often ideological view of the interplay between these mechanisms sustain this void of knowledge and expertise.

Not only anticipating change has been proven hard for the academic disciplines, but also formulating answers. Often, the policies, plans and procedures that emerge as answers fail because they do not fit the present situation, the present manners of coordinating policies and practices, or, conversely, because they see new situations too much in the light of old stories embedded in governance structures. It is therefore surprising that little attention has been paid to governance evolution, its processes, driving forces and mechanisms. Evolutionary Governance Theory (EGT) presents a new and cohesive perspective. Certain problems can be more easily anticipated in certain governance paths, and these paths yield certain answers more readily than others. EGT builds upon concepts and approaches from many disciplines: economics, public administration, sociology, anthropology, philosophy, political science, history and cultural studies. Institutional and development economics, social systems theory and post- structuralism provide key structural elements for a conceptual architecture that is both novel and unique, capable of pushing other theories further and able to provide new answers to pressing policy questions.

The focus of this book is governance, which is not a new phenomenon. In making collectively binding decisions, there were always more players than the government. Many players were involved in the Middle Ages, at the height of the absolutist state, and many players are involved now. Although the shift from government to governance has sometimes been presented as a dramatic break with a past, supposedly dominated by centralized governments, their bureaucracies, laws, policies and plans, it has to be understood in more subtle terms, disregarding the

K. Van Assche et al., *Evolutionary Governance Theory*, SpringerBriefs in Economics,
DOI: 10.1007/978-3-319-00984-1_1, © The Author(s) 2014

older self- presentations of modernist states as capable of creating transparency in society and capable of steering and social engineering (Luhmann 1997; Pierre and Peters 2000; Rhodes 1996; Scott 1998).

The same goes for another dominant discourse in public administration and related disciplines, the discourse on citizen participation as a panacea for the evils of government and market (Dryzek 2000; Fischer 2009; Forester 1999; Van Assche 2008; Van Assche et al. 2011). This discourse can best be understood as existing under the spell of similar self- presentations of late modernist governments. Citizens were always there, and the slowly evolved mechanisms of representative democracy did not erase the citizen. Rather, it looks like the semantics of democracy and market have changed for many citizens and scientific observers alike, making the structures and processes of representative democracy feel alien and creating a perception of its tools as either powerless or oppressive. Concurrently, making citizens feel just as alienated from markets, powerless against their forces, supposedly unleashed in a neo-liberal age of small government.

In parallel, a critique of law, policies and plans, developed in several disciplines (Allmendinger 2001; Pressman and Wildavsky 1979; Beunen 2010). These governmental tools were presented as either oppressive weapons of the rich and powerful, or as powerless tools of governments incapable of adapting to new evolutions (Scott 1985; Kornai and Rose-Ackerman 2004). At the same time, many critics of neo-liberal market regimes, of their environmental effects, their undermining of local democracy and self- organization, call again for new and better laws, policies and plans. A large part of the scientific community (except for economists) seems to dislike markets, especially global markets (Leman 2000). Yet these researchers seem to have a very ambiguous relation with government, as foe and ally, a relation perfused with nostalgia perhaps for the ideal of a high modernist state somehow enlightened by science. This time a science of environmental justice, a science of fair economic relations and of local democracy. Luckily, the scientific community is not homogeneous and many alternative visions of current and desirable political economies emerged in various disciplines.

This book is based on a long period of investigation and experimentation, of fieldwork and theoretical reflection, spanning three continents and a number of disciplines. It is an introduction and a work in progress, a call for and an example of what we call *Evolutionary Governance Theory*, or *EGT*. We intend to present a new mapping of the terrain between libertarian approaches to government and social engineering thinking, between mythologies of entirely free markets producing an optimal organization of society and mythologies of central planning materializing utopian dreams. Both approaches we deem mythical because they start from ideological premises, rather than from analyses of governance and governance effects (cf. Machiavelli 1988). Insight in variations in markets and democracies, and in the evolutions producing these variations, we consider of the utmost practical and theoretical importance.

An evolutionary perspective is necessary because the effects of governance arrangements are always influenced by the dynamic networks of actors, discourses, and institutions. Various authors have shown how formal institutions evolved from informal ones and that these informal institutions sustain, modify, undermine, reinforce, and complement formal institutions (Greif 2006; North 2005; Ligrom et al. 1990). The implementation histories of laws, plans and policies cannot be understood without reference to this informality. What we need to understand is how organizations, perspectives and institutions are continuously changing in relation to each other. Reflection on versions of democracy then, ought to include not only descriptions of differences in organizational structures and formal institutions, but also of the interweaving of formal and informal (Van Assche et al. 2012a). Since the essence of democracy probably lies in the presence of rules of self-transformation, rules to change the rules, the identity of a polity can be seen as the configuration of formal and informal institutions ruling its self-transformation. It also means that a pattern of evolution becomes visible as the essence of a political community.

Similar observations can be made regarding markets. Many versions of markets exist, depending on formal structures, on specific linkages with law, politics, maybe science, but also based on different relations between formal and informal coordination mechanisms for market transactions. Markets were formed in the same networks of informality as political structures, developed in many forms, shaped by informality and by relations with politics and law (Greif 2006). Understanding the diversity of governance and market forms requires thus an understanding of the histories of their makings, an evolutionary perspective.

Variations in markets and democracies, and in their evolutions have produced many different governance systems (North et al. 2009; Ostrom 2005). Understanding variations and evolutions can help theory and practice to develop a more critical distance from perspectives presenting a stark choice between 'big or small' government or between 'the' free market or 'the state'. Many markets and many forms of government are possible. Many linkages are possible, between law, economy and politics, and many configurations of formal and informal institutions can be found in practice. Recognizable markets emerged in evolutions that simultaneously shaped rules (institutions), roles (actors), and the organizations embodying these roles and embodying specific linkages between economic, political and legal domains.

EGT thus understands governance as radically evolutionary: all elements of governance are subject to evolution, they co-evolve, and most of them are the product of governance itself. The perspective creates new spaces of analysis and new spaces for and modes of intervention. It also envisions new limitations to intervention. The dichotomy between market and state might dissolve and new variations are likely to occur. Yet one cannot simply redesign a capitalist democracy, nor any other regime, or any other linkage between economic and political domains (Allina–Pisano 2008; Verdery 2003). One cannot jump from each branch in the evolutionary tree to each imaginable other branch. Evolutions are marked by dependency.

After introducing the theoretical antecedents of the theory in the next chapters, and the essential building blocks, we will reflect on these policy implications of EGT.

References

Allina–Pisano, J. (2008). *Post soviet potemkin villages. Politics and property rights in the black earth*. Cambridge: Cambridge University Press.
Allmendinger, P. (2001). *Planning in postmodern times*. London: Routledge.
Beunen, R. (2010). *The governance of nature: How nature conservation ambitions have been dashed in planning practices*. Wageningen: Wageningen University.
Dryzek, J. (2000). *Deliberative democracy and beyond*. Oxford: Oxford University Press.
Fischer, F. (2009). *Democracy and expertise: Reorienting policy inquiry*. Oxford: Oxford University Press.
Forester, J. (1999). *The deliberative practitioner. Encouraging participatory planning processes*. Cambridge: MIT Press.
Greif, A. (2006). *Institutions and the path to the modern economy: lessons from medieval trade*. Cambridge: Cambridge University Press.
Kornai, J., & Rose-Ackerman, S. (Eds.). (2004). *Building a trustworthy state in post-socialist transition*. New York: Palgrave.
Leman, J. (Ed.). (2000). *The dynamics of emerging ethnicities: Immigrant and indigenous ethnogenesis in confrontation*. Frankfurt: Peter Land.
Ligrom, P., North, D., & Weingast, B. (1990). The role of institutions in the revival of trade: The law merchant, private judges and the champagine fairs. *Economics and Politics, 2*(1), 1–23.
Luhmann, N. (1997). *Die gesellschaft der gesellschaft*. Frankfurt: Suhrkamp.
Machiavelli, N. (1988). *The prince*. Cambridge: Cambridge University Press.
North, D., Wallis, J., & Weingast, B. (2009). *Violence and social orders. a conceptual framework for interpreting recorded human history*. Cambridge: Cambrigde University Press.
North, D. C. (2005). *Understanding the process of economic change*. Princeton: Princeton University Press.
Ostrom, E. (2005). *Understanding institutional diversity*. Princeton: Princeton University Press.
Pierre, J., & Peters, B. G. (2000). *Governance, politics, and the state*. Basingstoke: Macmillan.
Pressman, J. L., & Wildavsky, A. B. (1979). *Implementation: How great expectations in Washington are dashed in Oakland* (2d edn.). Berkeley: University of California Press.
Rhodes, R. A. W. (1996). The new governance: Governing without government. *Political Studies, 44*(4), 652–667.
Scott, J. C. (1985). *Weapons of the weak: Everyday forms of peasant resistance*. New Haven: Yale University Press.
Scott, J. C. (1998). *Seeing like a state: How certain schemes to improve the human condition have failed*. New Haven: Yale University Press.
Van Assche, K. (2008). *Va'Amenez- nous les citoyens et incluez-les!' Les chemins tortueux de la participation citoyenne dans les theories et les pratiques de l'urbanisme contemporain*. In M. Hubert & F. Delmotte (Eds.), *La cite administrative de l'etat a la croisee des chemins. Des enjeux pour la ville et l'action publique a Bruxelles*. Brussels: Editions La Cambre.
Van Assche, K., Beunen, R., & Duineveld, M. (2012a). *Formal/informal dialectics and the self-transformation of spatial planning systems: An exploration*. Administration and Society (online first).
Van Assche, K., Duineveld, M., Beunen, R., & Teampau, P. (2011). Delineating locals: Transformations of knowledge/power and the governance of the Danube Delta. *Journal of Environmental Policy and Planning, 13*(1), 1–21.
Verdery, K. (2003). *The vanishing hectare: Property and value in postsocialist Transylvania*. Ithaca: Cornell University Press.

Part II
Governance as Evolution

Chapter 2
Theoretical Sources of EGT

Abstract In this chapter we outline the main theoretical sources of EGT-social systems theory, new institutional economics, development economics, and post-structuralism in different versions.

2.1 Biological Theories of Evolution

Evolution in EGT perspective is a process of creating and weeding out variations. It is a process of creating new variations out of older ones, of gradual emergence and hardening of structure out of flow, and of gradual transformation of that structure in continued evolution (cf. Stichweh 2000; Luhmann 1997). We describe EGT as a radically evolutionary perspective since we consider everything a product of evolution, both elements and structures, their interaction and the rules of transformation. Thus, in governance, we consider rules (institutions), roles (actors) and organizations (embodying roles), their interactions and their transformation rules as the result of evolution. They are impossible to comprehend without reference to evolution. Yet, not everything can be explained by reference to evolutions internal to governance.

EGT is indebted at an elementary level to biological evolutionary theory, more specifically to the version developed by Francisco Varela and Humberto Maturana, two biologists (Maturana and Varela 1987). They conceived the idea of *autopoiesis*, wherein everything in an biological system is the product of the evolution of that system. One cannot logically refer to the environment to explain observed features. What is present in a cell for example, the elements of a cell, the biochemical processes, the system of reproduction, has to be explained as the result of the process of reproduction of the cell, using the existing elements and procedures. If the cell would be open to direct interference from the environment, it would dissolve into separate elements. Its reproduction would come to a halt and it could no longer be called a cell. For Varela and Maturana, autopoiesis therefore entails

K. Van Assche et al., *Evolutionary Governance Theory*, SpringerBriefs in Economics, DOI: 10.1007/978-3-319-00984-1_2, © The Author(s) 2014

operational closure: the reproduction of the cell rests on a set of operations that is entirely internal to the cell. The environment has *influence* in various ways, e.g. by generating inputs for processes in the cell, but what counts as input and how it is processed, is defined in and by the cell alone. Environments are always interpreted in and by the system, never dictate adaptation in a certain manner. The schemes of interpretation are themselves a product of evolution.

2.2 Social Systems Theory

Niklas Luhmann, the father of social systems theory, borrowed the concepts of autopoiesis and operational closure from Varela and Maturana (Luhmann 1989; Maturana and Varela 1987). Over three decades he built a theory of society that can be considered the most important foundation of EGT (Luhmann 1995, 2000, 2004). Varela and Maturana had tried to modify their theory into a theory of society, but it was Luhmann's stroke of genius to identify neither people nor actions as the elements of an autopoietic theory of society, but *communications* (Luhmann 1989). Social systems (according to Luhmann) are nothing else than on-going processes of interpretation and reinterpretation of internal and external environments.

Luhmann sees society as a population of social systems that is becoming ever more abundant. He distinguishes three categories of social systems. Firstly, *interactions* (conversations), these are fleeting systems with a limited capacity to process environmental complexity. Secondly, *organizations*, these are social systems with clear boundaries reproducing themselves by means of decisions. Thirdly, *function systems, these* are systems that are not delineated by membership but by the specificity of their perspective. Law, economy, politics, religion, science and education are examples of function systems that each play a role in the reproduction of society as the encompassing social system. A function system reproduces itself by applying distinct codes, thereby maintaining a boundary vis-à-vis other function systems. Law sees reality according to schemes grounded in the distinction legal/illegal, science deploys the distinction true/untrue, economy calculates in terms of value/no value, while politics operates by means of the distinction power/powerless.

All social systems are self-referential. Each social system internally produces a construction of itself and the outside world, that is, other social systems and the world at large, in terms of unique basic distinctions, concepts and procedures and it recursively produces its communications from the network of its communications (Teubner 1989). Each social system reproduces itself by means of internal elements, by means of and in reference to earlier concepts, distinctions, and procedures. Therewith social systems theory offers a theoretical framework to analyse the communicative processes that shape historically contingent social practices of discourse (social systems) that produce the criteria for their own transformation (Luhmann 1995, 2004; Teubner 1988).

Luhmann himself did not appreciate the term post-modernism, but leans for his epistemology on a tradition of German radical constructivists for whom 'reality' is a by-product of observation (Glasersfeld 1995). *Hetero-reference* is possible, and necessary for society to function as more than a set of unrelated subsystems, yet it is always grounded in self- reference. Each object, subject, action, narrative, perceived in the environment is perceived and interpreted according to the schemes of the system. The environment includes other social systems, other function systems, organizations and interactions.

A second consequence of Luhmann's choice for communications as the elements of social systems is that communication loses its transparency that was so important to political philosophers since enlightenment and that grounded so many theories of politics and governance, from Locke and Montesquieu to Habermas and the proponents of participation (King and Tornhill 2006). Social systems for Luhmann are cognitively open yet operationally closed; they continuously learn from their environment, yet under their own conditions. The post-enlightenment assumption of communication as a potentially transparent connection between two individuals, and by extension, a fabric unifying the political community and enabling fair decision-making, is shattered in a social systems perspective. People participate in communication. If they want to talk to other people, if they want to share something of their experience, this is only possible by uttering something that will always mean something else for the other party because of the operational closure of communication, an autopoietic middle ground hovering in between two autopoietically closed minds (Luhmann 1995). The same applies to social systems: they cannot communicate directly to each other. Whatever happens in their environment, will be interpreted in terms of their own autopoietic identity, resting on a unique set of basic distinctions, interpretive procedures and semantics. Everything is interpretation, constant reinterpretation.

From a social systems point of view, it is important to stress that people as individuals exist in two ways, as ascriptions of this or that social system (where individual X in role Y is recognized) and as psychic systems, able to process meaning, that are part of the environment of social systems. People and social systems co-evolved, as each other's preferred and necessary environment. People and systems always remain partly opaque to each other and will respond to steering attempts in ways that are not entirely predictable. This, for Luhmann, is not a problem, but a precondition for the development and functioning of complex societies (King and Thornhill 2003; Luhmann 1997).

2.3 Post-structuralism

Post-structuralism means many things to many people. We understand it as a constructivist epistemology, a manifest for analysis of governance as a meeting ground of different worlds. Governance appears as a process wherein worlds collide, fight for pre-eminence, mutate, transform, and recombine. Governance absorbs, reflects, and creates realities. The post-structualist works by Michel Foucault, Roland Barthes (Barthes 1957; Foucault 1972, 1994) Jacques Lacan (Lacan and Fink 2006;

Haute 2002), Jacques Derrida (Derrida 1967, 1972, 1973), Bruno Latour (Latour and Woolgar 1986; Latour 1999) and Gilles Deleuze (Deleuze and Guattari 1987, 1994; Deleuze and Howard 2000) have much to offer for the understanding of governance, and will be selectively mined in the following chapters. For each of these theorists, a substantial literature has developed in various disciplines, with different accents and biases, and different degrees of closure to other disciplines and theorists. We cannot highlight each version of Foucault or any of the other authors on the market, but will indicate which one is on our shelf and why.

Foucault, among the post-structuralists, is most important for the construction of EGT. We will adopt several Foucaultian concepts and insights into our conceptual framework. First of all, *discourse*. In line with Foucault, we consider a discourse a structured set of concepts that enables access to a certain part or aspect of reality, while simultaneously veiling other parts or aspects (Foucault 1972, 1994; cf. Howarth 2000). Reality as a whole and reality as an ultimate ground cannot be known. Foucault never denied the existence of something outside discourse, but as soon as we reason, observe or communicate, we are within discourse. What we do, is also structured by discourse. Actions, movements, in their observation but also in their execution are never free of structuring linked to discursive structures.

Discourses develop and deploy structure at different levels. Discourses develop concepts, objects and subjects, which can lead autonomous lives, gain prominence, migrate, return and modify broader discursive contexts. They can have narrative structures, including characters, events, episodes, heroes and villains, lulls and dramatic climaxes. Narratives can be embedded in ideologies, explaining the world at large, ways to organize a polity and way to live in it. Ideologies can revolve around metaphors, shedding a new light on the world, and metaphors can be nested in other metaphors, using a similar angle of observation.

Discourses, in an EGT perspective, are self-referential, just as with Luhmann, in the sense that they construct the world by means of references to their own elements, and in the sense that new structures are always grounded in prior ones. Discourses evolve. They transform in the on-going processes by which they recursively reproduce themselves, but this transformation is governed by its self-referentiality. One can therefore speak of operational closure and of autopoiesis (Teubner 1989). At this level discourse theory is compatible with social systems theory. One can draw the parallel with systems theory further, and point out that, for Foucault, but also e.g. Lacan, everything said about the discursive world at large can be mirrored at the smaller scale of one discourse, and that moving between discourses requires crossing gaps that cannot be closed discursively (Haute 2002). The discursive mechanisms analysed by the other post-structuralists, and many of the concepts they developed for that purpose, can then be imported in the developing frame of EGT. We will see that Roland Barthes' insights on discursive migration, on metaphor and ideology (Barthes 1957), can acquire a new productivity within an EGT frame, and we will resort to Jacques Lacan for the analysis of open concepts (Kooij et al. 2013), very generic concepts enabling the reproduction of governance by glossing over differences between world-construction of between discourses.

2.4 Institutional and Development Economics

Social systems theory and post-structuralism can thus be combined in the development of an evolutionary perspective on governance since each theory is starting from a world that consists of interpretations, a world that is in constant movement, where interpretations are competing and evolving. These theoretical worlds leave room for people, for the agency of individuals and groups. It is just that individuals and groups, in their agency, and in their observation of other groups and individuals and their agency, can never escape the power and the autonomy of communication, of discourse (Van Assche et al. 2011). A conversation between groups in a governance situation is necessarily a web of interpretations, within each group, between the groups, probably in the context of an organizational setting that further frames what happens. It will be a web that incorporates existing ascriptions of self, others, actions, goals and almost certainly transforms some of those beyond the intentionality and/or comprehension of the speakers. As soon as something is said, it is subject to the mechanics of discourse, to metaphorical sliding, to distortions by the seeping in of utopias and dystopias, to entanglements with power that cannot be fully grasped.

Such assertions of the autonomy and the structured character of the discursive, of the autopoiesis and the operational closing of communication do not preclude that individual action can be structured and have effects. If we are interested in a theory of governance that is evolutionary and capable of envisioning a variety of alternatives in the relations between market and politics, we ought to add a perspective that can articulate economic and political agency in a way that accepts contingency and evolution, and allows for multiple realities and rationalities. Such theory exists, we believe, and we locate it in the fields of institutional economics and development economics.

We use the work of North (2005), Seabright (2010), Greif (2006), Eggertsson (2005), Acemoglu (2012), Easterly (2006) and Ostrom (2005) under this flag of institutional economics and development economics, while recognizing individual differences between them. We want to emphasize some highly interesting changes in these branches of economics, in the last decade, which makes them more interesting for the construction of EGT. *First of all*, a full articulation of a radically evolutionary perspective with many of these authors. For some, as for the late North, but also Greif and Seabright, this goes as far as acknowledging the co-evolution of rules (institutions), roles and organizations, the emergence of formal institutions out of informality, and the continued importance of informal institutions in the functioning of formal institutions. *Secondly*, these authors acknowledge the importance of politics and law for the structure and functioning of markets, beyond a mere nod to the 'rule of law', assumed to be a unitary condition. Markets are embedded in other institutions, and have effects because of them. *Thirdly*, in this new approach the diversity of market arrangements and coordination mechanisms becomes observable as more than deviations from, or steps towards a 'free' market. Different market forms, linked to different forms of political and legal organization, are interpreted as results of different evolutions (within the economic domain) and co-evolutions (with law and politics).

Fourthly, gradually, North, Greif, Seabright and Eggertsson discovered that, since both value and transaction costs are culturally constructed and the relation between formal and informal coordination differs per culture and community, *what appears as rational and real* is not a unified construct.

These economists do not engage with post-structuralism or social systems theory. Their investigations often started with small-scale observations or historical studies of interactions on early or less developed markets. In their investigations they figured out, as some others did in geography, anthropology, public administration and policy studies, that structure and agency are indeed in a dialectical relation, mutually shaping each other. More importantly they observed that structuring of action results from both discourse and previous action, and that no logic of action (e.g. of rational market behaviour) can be distilled independent of discourse. Furthermore they show that discourses in non-economic domains, as well as the organizational structure of these domains (such as law and politics), influence both action and discourse in the economic domain. These insights make it possible to combine this branch of economics with social systems theory and post- structuralism in the construction of EGT.

Social systems theory, developed in the 1980s and 1990s, post-structuralism, from the 1970s and 1980s, but applied in governance studies more recently, and the institutional economics that appeared after 2000, enable us to present a picture of evolving governance. The concepts introduced are not enough to spell out the possible permutations of elements stemming from these theories. And they are not EGT itself. What has been said allows us to grasp however, that this can be a basis on which to build a perspective that allows us to see governance as radically evolutionary, as driven by actions and ideas, as acting on images of self, environment, past and future, that are evolving themselves.

In the following chapters, we will dwell less on these three foundational theories and focus on the construction of EGT. Additional elements derived from the foundational theories will be incorporated, often modified, and their provenance will be mentioned. Many other concepts and insights are new, as is the structure of EGT itself. Yet other ideas have still different origins, ranging from Aristotle over Machiavelli to landscape ecology, planning theory and semiotics. We gradually work towards a clarification of the emergent order of EGT, as an autonomous theory incorporating elements of various origin (Chap. 9). The next step (Chap. 3) stays recognizably rooted in systems theory and institutional economics. We discuss functional and organizational differentiation, formal, informal and dead institutions, and recombine these old and new concepts in a new manner to give more detail to our concept of evolution. This more developed concept will then allow us in Chap. 4 to analyse governance paths.

References

Acemoglu, D., & Robinson, J. (2012). *Why nations fail. The origins of power, prosperity and poverty*. New York: Crown Business.

Barthes, R. (1957). *Mythologies*. Paris: Éditions du Seuil.

Deleuze, G., & Guattari, F. (1987). *A thousand plateaus: Capitalism and schizophrenia*. London: Continuum.

Deleuze, G., & Guattari, F. (1994). *What is philosophy?* New York: Columbia University Press.
Deleuze, G., & Howard, R. (2000). *Proust and signs: The complete text*. London: Athlone.
Derrida, J. (1967). *De la grammatologie*. Paris: Editions de Minuit.
Derrida, J. (1972). *La dissémination*. Paris: Editions du Seuil.
Derrida, J. (1973). *Speech and phenomena, and other essays on Husserl's theory of signs*. Evanston: Northwestern University Press.
Easterly, W. (2006). *The white man's burden: Why the West's efforts to aid the rest have done so much ill and so little good*. Oxford: Oxford University Press.
Eggertsson, T. (2005). *Imperfect institutions: Possibilities and limits of reform*. Ann Arbor: University of Michigan Press.
Foucault, M. (1972). *The archaeology of knowledge & the discourse on language*. New York: Pantheon Books.
Foucault, M. (1994). Truth and juridical forms. In J. D. Faubion (Ed.), *Power. Essential works of Foucault 1954–1984* (Vol. 3, pp. 1–89). New York: The New Press.
von Glasersfeld, E. (1995). *Radical constructivism: A way of knowing and learning*. London: Falmer Press.
Greif, A. (2006). *Institutions and the path to the modern economy: Lessons from medieval trade*. Cambridge: Cambridge University Press.
Haute, P. v. (2002). *Against adaptation: Lacan's "subversion" of the subject*. New York: Other Press.
Howarth, D. (2000). *Discourse*. Buckingham: Open University Press.
King, M., & Thornhill, E. (2003). *Niklas Luhmann's theory of politics and law*. Basingstoke: Palgrave Macmillan.
King, M., & Tornhill, C. (Eds.). (2006). *Luhmann on law and politics. Critical appraisals and applications*. Oxford: Hart.
Kooij, H., Van Assche, K., & Lagendijk, A. (2013). Open concepts as crystallization points and enablers of discursive configurations: The case of the innovation campus in the Nether-lands. *European Planning Studies, Online First*.
Lacan, J., & Fink, B. (2006). *Ecrits: The first complete edition in English*. New York: W.W. Norton & Co.
Latour, B. (1999). *Pandora's hope: Essays on the reality of science studies*. London: Harvard University Press.
Latour, B., & Woolgar, S. (1986). *Laboratory life: The construction of scientific facts*. Princeton, N.J.: Princeton University Press.
Luhmann, N. (1989). *Ecological communication*. Chicago: University of Chicago Press.
Luhmann, N. (1995). *Social systems*. Stanford: Stanford University Press.
Luhmann, N. (1997). *Die gesellschaft der gesellschaft*. Frankfurt: Suhrkamp.
Luhmann, N. (2000). *Art as a social system*. Stanford: Stanford University Press.
Luhmann, N. (2004). *Law as a social system*. Oxford: Oxford University Press.
Maturana, H. R., & Varela, F. J. (1987). *The tree of Knowledge. The biological roots of human understanding*. Boston: Shambhala Publications.
North, D. C. (2005). *Understanding the process of economic change*. Princeton: Princeton University Press.
Ostrom, E. (2005). *Understanding institutional diversity*. Princeton: Princeton University Press.
Seabright, P. (2010). *The company of strangers: A natural history of economic life*. Princeton: Princeton University Press.
Stichweh, R. (2000). *Die weltgesellschaft. Soziologische analysen*. Frankfurt: Suhrkamp.
Teubner, G. (Ed.). (1988). *Autopoietic Law: A new approach to law and society*. Berlin: Walter de Gruyter.
Teubner, G. (1989). How the Law Thinks: Towards a Constructivist Epistemology of Law. *Law & Society Review, 23*, 727–758.
Van Assche, K., Duineveld, M., Beunen, R., & Teampau, P. (2011). Delineating locals: Transformations of knowledge/power and the governance of the danube delta. *Journal of Environmental Policy and Planning, 13*(1), 1–21.

Chapter 3
Foundational Concepts

Abstract In this chapter we present some foundational concepts of EGT. We elaborate on functional and organisational differentiation and on formal, informal and dead institutions. The way these two sets of concepts are combined, forms the basis of our perspective on governance paths.

3.1 Functional Differentiation

The idea of *functional differentiation* is not new. Many theorists noticed of course that things change, that societies evolve, and within societies new roles, functions, organizations, groups emerge, while others disappear. We borrow the version of Luhmann and social systems theory, but functional differentiation in some form or other has been theorized by a series of others, from Max Weber and Emile Durkheim to Talcott Parsons, social historians and early systems theorists (Luhmann 2010). Usually, European history starting in the middle ages is the field of observation (Luhmann 2004). These authors saw a process of functional differentiation in the development of cities, in the combined revival of trade and local self-governance, and in the rise of learning (Seabright 2010; Greif 2006). These developments took place in organized forms, of slow separation of functional domains in society that made it possible to move to a next level of complexity. They also noticed that these processes are entwined. Self-governance made it possible to find levels of taxation, but also community investment that could benefit trade. Specialized and independent judges were better equipped to deal with trade conflicts and thus helped to expand trade. Some degree of literacy helped book-keeping and once specialized book-keepers existed, this spurred financial innovation, broadened the scope of transactions, increased demands on commercial law, caused innovation there et cetera, ad infinitum.

The separation of functional domains-law, science, economy, education, religion and politics tends to reinforce itself (Luhmann 1990). Once functions start to separate, dynamics starts that are hard to reverse, except of course by conquest

K. Van Assche et al., *Evolutionary Governance Theory*, SpringerBriefs in Economics, DOI: 10.1007/978-3-319-00984-1_3, © The Author(s) 2014

or collapse. It can be described in many ways, since it has many faces: separation of powers, independence of courts, free market, specialization and division of labour. None of those is entirely correct nor capable of fully grasping the process, but this is not surprising, since 'functional differentiation' is probably an overly ambitious concept. It tries to grasp the essence of change in western societies, a process of systemic change leading into eighteenth century enlightenment and the level of functional differentiation we call modernity. It is also, for the same reason, a highly abstract concept, so its empirical manifestations are likely to be diverse. Once domains start to separate, functional differentiation takes over from other forms of differentiation. It can replace *hierarchical differentiation*, based on a centre-periphery relation and an ideal of overview and control by a political centre. It can also replace *segmentary differentiation*, a catch phrase for many premodern societies structured along lines of clans, ethnic groups, extended families and tribes (Luhmann 1990).

Empirically, functional differentiation is never finished, and this has two meanings: the function systems seem to create new subsystems all the time. In science, new disciplines see the light every few years, in the economy, new sectors create their niche. Secondly, it means that no society is differentiated in only one manner. Modern societies might rely on functional differentiation for their reproduction, relegating politics to politicians, law to lawyers, commerce to merchants. Yet, traces of hierarchical and segmentary differentiation are almost certain to exist.

Luhmann modified the idea of functional differentiation, and made it a corner stone of his theory of social systems. For him too, in European history the function systems law, economy, politics, science and religion differentiated and slowly created their own autonomy and stable differences and relations. In his society of systems of communication, however, autonomy and stabilization mean autopoietic closure and drawing of system boundaries (Luhmann 1995). For him, functional differentiation entails the formation of a specific logic of reproduction within each system. Such logic is based on the unique application of unique procedures of observation, grounded in unique basic distinctions. Each function reconstructs the whole world internally, simplified according to the schemes grounded in that basic distinction. E.g. Law, as a social system, is not a collection of people, or even organizations, but a perspective on the world wherein everything is reduced to the distinction legal/illegal (Blomley 2008; Luhmann 2004; Teubner 1988). One can say that law, and the other function systems, create an internal construction of the world that enables it to maintain a narrow focus, a focus appertaining to a specialized role.

In social systems theory literally everything changes in evolution. That first of all refers to systems that evolve in their autopoietic reproduction, but it also implies that the way different systems relate to each other is evolving. Since social systems are autopoietic their relation to other social systems, which are in the environment of the social system, always depends on their own interpretations of those other systems. Social systems do not communicate with each other, but only about each other. The only mode to interact is based on their internal construction of reality and their own operations. Still interactions can take many forms and communications in one systems can trigger interpretations and changes in another system. Luhmann speaks of irritations (Luhmann 2004). Indirect responses are possible since changes in the environment of a certain social system, e.g. changes caused by other social systems, might cause 'irritations' that are produced within the social system itself. Irritations can be accidental or occur more regularly. In the case of recurrent and continuous mutual irritations between social systems we can speak of *structural couplings*. These are specific mechanisms that decide the duration, quality, intensity and institutionalisation of the link between different social systems (Luhmann 2004; Teubner 1989). Due to these structural couplings, events (communications) in one system act as an irritation for another social system and set off new events and communications there. In Luhmann's words (Luhmann 2004, p. 382): 'coupling mechanisms are called structural couplings if a system presupposes certain features of its environment on an on-going basis and relies on them structurally'.

Next to the mechanisms of self-steering and self-transformation in each function system, the pattern of couplings between systems creates a space for change and for possible intervention (Beunen and Van Assche 2013). It does not mean that politics could define a perfect set of couplings between all the systems and implement them. Rather, one can say that several systems produce ideas on the coupling with others, and use what they know as the existing set of couplings to influence the others systems, without ever being sure of the result. One can add that organizations, interactions (categories of social systems) and also individuals (as psychic systems in the environment of social systems) can indirectly influence the pattern of structural couplings. We will come back to this.

The manner in which especially law, politics and economy are coupled, creates different forms of regime, of democracy, of market, and leaves different spaces for policy and planning. This reiterates one of the points made earlier: *the* democracy and *the* market do not exist. One can distinguish a set of models of democracy, to categorize post hoc the results of different evolutionary paths. Yet, simple observation of the variety of markets and polities, of 'rules of law', and of the different modalities in which these domains can stabilize or destabilize each other, leaves no room for unified models that ought to represent the ideal outcome of evolution. If we subscribe to the theory of functional differentiation, there is a normative building block for EGT to be found: *some* form of functional differentiation has evolutionary advantages, some form of autopoietic closure of function systems enables specialization, and this makes it easier for society as a whole to become better at more things.

Differentiation has advantages and disadvantages. It enables the processing of environmental complexity by creating complex internal models and it stabilizes specialized interaction, e.g. commercial transactions. Yet it also represents risk and instability. Politics loses its overview and control of society. The other function systems are partly opaque to its observation and partly insensitive to its steering attempts (Van Assche and Verschraegen 2008). Furthermore there is the always lurking danger of *de-differentiation*: of losing the advantages of truly different perspectives and their interaction. De-differentiation can be more than a throwback to a previous stage of evolution. If a powerful state apparatus developed under the aegis of functional differentiation, with supposedly separation of powers, independent courts, religion and science, but de facto, a Stalinist-style regime is in charge, the powers unleashed by such state are potentially much more destructive than those of the village society that might have existed before.

3.2 Organizational Differentiation

Functional differentiation took place together with, and thanks to, organizational differentiation. The two forms of differentiation supported each other, and they formed the substrate for each other. Specialized organizations made functional differentiation more likely and vice versa (Luhmann 1995). In medieval cities, specialized merchant's guilds, craftsmen's guilds, archery associations, semi-religious fraternities, *béguinages*, religious orders and other organizations dramatically furthered specialization, and enabled the self-governance of cities, while contributing to the expansion of trade and city life itself (Greif 2006).

Local self-governance in the early cities and later centralization of power in early modern nation states can be seen as part and parcel of the same process, combining functional and organizational differentiation. Centralization seems at odds with local self-governance, but the increased scale of states, the new networks of infrastructure, consistency of legal and political regimes over large territories, increased the scope of transactions. Conversely, most nation states were aware they had to foster trade and negotiate with cities before raising taxes or infringing on freedoms. In a similar way international cooperation, both by national governments and organizations contribute to the formation of a world society, in which national and ethnic boundaries are systematically disregarded in the reproduction of most function systems (Stichweh 2000).

What applies to function systems also applies to organizations: they are partly opaque to each other, and for themselves. They have a logic of reproduction that differs from the way they describe themselves (Seidl 2005). Organizations produce images of themselves and their environment, which includes for example competitors, customers, and political contexts. These images will always be incomplete. The environment is always internally reconstructed, an interpretation made by the organisation. Also the self, the exact nature of its autopoietic logic cannot be observed by the organisation in its entirety. It is logically impossible to observe a system from within the system. Self-observation also relies on images produced in the system, according to its own, partly invisible procedures. Organizations thus navigate their environment guided by self-descriptions that are always partial and descriptions of the environment that are never entirely adequate. Neither the environment nor its own behaviour is predictable.

Organizations are embedded in several function systems. A company, as a business organization, might have as it primary goal to make money, and to process information based on the distinction making/losing money, but the nature of its autopoiesis is that of an organization, not that of the function system economy.

It reproduces itself by means of decisions, and the structure of the decision-premises is the result of the history of the organization, the images of self and environment, of goals and priorities, strengths and weaknesses that evolved in that autopoiesis (Seidl 2005). Decisions are taken based on an image of self that is delineated, that is different from other companies, that includes certain departments, persons, roles, procedures, membership rules, promotion rules and measures for success and failure. In other words, in decisions, many perspectives are already included, many activities, many social systems. At a more trivial level one can observe that different departments and roles combine different social systems. HRM might have educational aspects, R&D can be semi-autonomous, and pursue scientific truth for most of the trajectory, while management is involved in external politics and making a career is essentially internal politics.

For the understanding of evolving governance, functional differentiation and organizational differentiation are utterly useful concepts. Understanding governance evolutions is in a very real sense understanding the path of this double differentiation and understanding the resulting patterns of structural couplings between function systems and linkages between organizations. Organizations do represent and contribute to the coupling of function systems. Different court systems (sets of organizations), including different roles for juries, lawyers, different procedures for appointment of judges (more or less politicized), different specializations of law firms (focusing e.g. more or less on property rights), represent different coupling between law, politics and economy. And the presence of such web of organizations will shape the further path of functional differentiation.

3.3 Formal/Informal and Dead Institutions

Governance takes place in a world that is dynamic. New semantics can emerge at any time, undermining the desirability of narratives embedded in governance, their believability, the trust between actors, and trust in the stability and value of the objects structuring governance. A wide variety of actors can play a role in governance, as individuals and organizations. The coordination of this variety of actors in order to develop collectively binding decisions, is difficult. If we accept that governance evolves in a complex and unstable world, incorporating changing combinations of actors, expertise, world-views, it is unlikely that coordination can rely on stable rules for a long time. As coordinative mechanisms, rules are continuously evolving, in relation to other changes in society.

To understand the role of rules we come back to the idea of institutions mentioned before. We see institutions, in line with institutional economics, as rules of the game, as coordinative tools (Van Assche and van Biesebroeck 2013; North 2005; Ostrom 1990). The players of the game can be individuals or organizations, governmental and non-governmental, for profit and non-for profit. In governance, coordination is important to come to collective decisions. These decisions produce rules to guide decision-making proper, rules on how to deal with each other, rules of inclusion and exclusion of actors, expertise, topics and ideas in the process. Collective decisions can also produce rules to change each of these rules (Eggertsson 2005).

Democracy is essentially about rules to change the rules, about transformation options, and therefore this form of coordination requires analysis. It seems logical that inclusion of more actors and ideas, and more governance experiment, will only increase the focus on these transformation rules, and hence the constant redefinition of democratic forms. It also seems logical that anxiety can easily take over in a community, when new governance forms differ significantly from what was recognized as 'democratic'. One can also surmise that some governance experiments, including new forms of citizen participation, inspired fear because the relation with existing rules of transformation (and representation) was not thought out well (Van Assche et al. 2011b).

In the naturally unstable environment of governance, all rules can come under scrutiny, can be disputed, and this source of instability joins the source already mentioned: the seeping in of alternative visions, valuations and desires from elsewhere. We can combine this with the ideas on informality presented earlier. Formal coordination mechanisms have effects because of informal institutions they are embedded in and formal and informal institutions reshape each other continuously (Van Assche et al. 2012, 2013; Guha-Khasnobis et al. 2007; North 2005; Ellickson 1991). Each source of instability can therefore affect both formal and informal institutions. The interactions of those institutions make the governance evolution even more unpredictable. If changing narratives for example undermine the attractiveness of a vision underpinning formal rules, these rules will lose their grip and their coordinative power. If power struggles in governance lead to a shift of formal rules, then groups that feel disenfranchised can start to disobey these new rules or sabotage the rule-making process.

Formal institutions are not only embedded in informality, but carry it as a shadow of alternative coordination options. Formality in our perspective is the result of a choice or decision made again in each situation where there are several coordination options. In such a situation one coordination option carries the weight of general expectation that makes it formality. The distinction between formal and informal is thus a labelling that takes place with each and every decision. In modern states, formality is regularly associated with the state, with rules written down on paper, and with state organizations, but this is not necessarily always the case. In modern governance, laws, policies, but also plans can play the role of formal institution.

We add a third type of institutions: dead institutions (Van Assche et al. 2012). These institutions were once considered formal, they are still on the books, but have no effects currently because they are not considered a real coordination option; yet the fact that they are on the books makes it possible to revive them. Dead institutions are thus the product of modern societies, and relevant for governance evolutions, as they can hark back to former stages in the evolution. They do not revive old times, but they can bring back some lost coupling between actors, lost objects, or give existing objects a new meaning and impact, renders some forgotten subjects relevant et cetera.

Formal and informal institutions co-evolve and cannot be entirely separated in analysis. The effects of formal institutions hinge on the existing informal institutions and the other way around. Dead institutions, once accumulated in a modern society with strong memory-mechanisms, render the interplay between institutions more complex (Van Assche et al. 2011a). They can be treated as an additional source of instability in evolving governance, but also an additional source of invention and experimentation, and therefore adaptation. Instead of assessing the results of formal institutions separately, when analysing governance and thinking of policy recommendations, we consider it better to think in terms of *configurations* of formal, informal and possibly dead institutions, and assess the results of these configurations in terms of public goods envisioned in the community. It should be said that the results of these configurations are not always visible, or immediately visible, or entirely visible. It is very well possible that outside observers focus on certain informalities undermining what they recognize as the rule of law, while missing the utility of informalities in the economic survival of certain groups, or in the furthering of public goods think for example of fire-fighters asking bribes from potential builders, and using the money just to do their job.

Formal, informal and dead institutions shape and are shaped by governance evolution. Their interplay can create stability and instability, conservatism and innovation. Structurally, change is always possible. Change can come from formal and informal histories of coordination, and at each point in these histories, discursive worlds can enter and reshape the course of evolution. An ideology can lose its luster, a community can become obsessed with cars, a person convinces a community that he is a leader, that a leader is a hero, and that changing some rules will bring glorious deeds. The concept of institutions thus directs the attention to the agency-aspect of evolution, and to the potential for governance reform by of different players and by changing rules. Our broadened concept of institutions, inspired by recent versions of institutional economics, creates room to think of the routes by which discursive shifts continuously alter the identity of actors, the explicit and implicit goals of governance, the impact of rules and the strategizing going on. It also enables us to link up with the radically constructivist perspective of social systems theory, and its concepts of functional and organizational differentiation.

Governance for us includes individuals and organizations that can become actors by participating in governance. Actors coordinate decision-making by means of institutions formal, informal and dead. Governance implies taking decisions, and given the plurality of actors and continuous changes in society, many different and ever changing versions of reality, of past, present and (desirable) future are continuously intervening in the *configuration of actors and institutions*. Both actors and institutions are remoulded in and by discursive dynamics. Sometimes actors are aware of this, in most cases they are not. 'Things have always been like this', might refer to an era of 3 years, beyond which their social memory does not span.

Insofar as actors are organizations, we consider them operationally closed (Seidl 2005). They are subjected to the inescapability of interpretation and reinterpretation systems theory ascribes to them. The unique logic of reproduction of each organization, their self-image, their decision procedures, what they consider their function and constituency, as success and failure, will inspire their strategizing in a governance arena. It will affect their perception of actors, institutions and the arena itself. Governance, as politics, is in its evolution further framed by the specific set of couplings that evolved between politics and the other function systems. Actor/institution configurations in governance, in their co-evolution, cannot escape the reigning configuration of structural couplings of law, economy and politics. 'Participation' cannot suddenly erase centuries of development towards representation in a community, with a specific version of representative democracy being coupled to a specific organization of the legal system and the market (Van Assche et al. 2011b). What we call *governance paths* in the following chapters, are governance evolutions framed by this structured set of forces.

References

Beunen, R., & Van Assche, K. (2013). Contested delineations: Planning, law and the governance of protected areas. *Environment and Planning A, 45*(6), 1285–1301.

Blomley, N. (2008). Enclosure, common right and the property of the the poor. *Social and Legal Studies, 17*(3), 311–331.

Eggertsson, T. (2005). *Imperfect institutions: possibilities and limits of reform.* Ann Arbor: University of Michigan Press.

Ellickson, R. (1991). *Order without law. How neighbors settle disputes.* Cambridge: Harvard University Press.

Greif, A. (2006). *Institutions and the path to the modern economy: Lessons from medieval trade.* Cambridge: Cambridge University Press.

Guha-Khasnobis, B., Kanbur, R., & Ostrom, E. (Eds.). (2007). *Linking the formal and informal economy. Concepts and policies.* Oxford: Oxford University Press.

Luhmann, N. (1990). *Political theory in the welfare state.* Berlin: Mouton de Gruyter.

Luhmann, N. (1995). *Social systems.* Stanford: Stanford University Press.

Luhmann, N. (2004). *Law as a social system.* Oxford: Oxford University Press.

Luhmann, N. (2010). *Introduction to systems theory.* Cambridge: Polity.

North, D. C. (2005). *Understanding the process of economic change.* Princeton: Princeton University Press.

Ostrom, E. (1990). *Governing the commons: the evolution of institutions for collective action.* Cambridge: Cambridge University Press.

Seabright, P. (2010). *The company of strangers: a natural history of economic life.* Princeton: Princeton University Press.

Seidl, D. (2005). *Organizational identity and self- transformation. An autopoietic perspective.* Aldershot: Ashgate.

Stichweh, R. (2000). *Die weltgesellschaft. Soziologische analysen.* Frankfurt: Suhrkamp.

Teubner, G. (1989). How the law thinks: Towards a constructivist epistemology of law. *Law & Society Review, 23*(5), 727–758.

Teubner, G. (Ed.). (1988). *Autopoietic Law: A new approach to law and society.* Berlin: Walter de Gruyter.

Van Assche, K., Beunen, R., & Duineveld, M. (2012). Formal/informal dialectics and the self-transformation of spatial planning systems: An exploration. *Administration & Society, Online First.*

Van Assche, K., Beunen, R., Jacobs, J., & Teampau, P. (2011a). Crossing trails in the marshes: rigidity and flexibility in the governance of the Danube Delta. *Journal of Environmental Planning and Management, 54*(8), 997–1018.

Van Assche, K., Duineveld, M., Beunen, R., & Teampau, P. (2011b). Delineating locals: Transformations of knowledge/power and the governance of the Danube Delta. *Journal of Environmental Policy & Planning, 13*(1), 1–21.

Van Assche, K., Shtaltovna, A., Hornidge, A. K. (2013). Visible and invisible informalities and institutional transformation. Lessons from transition countries: Georgia, Romania, Uzbekistan. In N. Hayoz & C. Giordano (Eds.), *Informality and post- socialist transition.* Frankfurt: Peter Lang.

Van Assche, K., & Van Biesebroeck, J. (2013). Governing the ice. Ice fishing villages on Lake Mille Lacs and he creation of environmental governance institutions. *Journal of Environmental Planning and Management, online first.*

Van Assche, K., & Verschraegen, G. (2008). The limits of planning: Niklas luhmann's systems theory and the analysis of planning and planning ambitions. *Planning Theory, 7*(3), 263–283.

Part III
Building Blocks for Evolutionary Governance Theory

Chapter 4
Evolutionary Paths

Abstract In this chapter we discuss the concept of governance paths and the forms of dependency marking paths. The forms of dependency constitute rigidities in governance evolution, but leave space for flexibility, for path creation.

4.1 Governance Paths

The specific evolution of governance in a community is referred to with the concept of a path. We already prepared this concept in the previous chapter, where we discussed elements and driving forces. Actors, institutions and expertise co-evolve in a governance evolution (Van Assche et al. 2011; North 2005; Van Assche and Djanibekov 2012). They form each other and are formed in and by governance processes. We now add that governance paths cross sites and display mechanisms. Sites are places and occasions of higher communicative density. They refer to times and places when and where decisions are taken or prepared, where within or between actors alternative courses of collective action are assessed. Mechanisms is a broad concept that includes institutions (as coordination mechanisms), mechanisms of object formation (see below) and stratagems, or individual actor's devices to influence the game. The inclusion of new actors can shift the path, can introduce new mechanisms into the game, which in return can be emulated by other actors.

Governance in modern society is multi-level governance, which means that several paths exist in a (larger) community. These paths can run parallel, they can entangle, and they can block each other. Evolutions in one path can affect the other paths, both positively and negatively, by inspiring conformity or by inspiring deviation. Actors can participate in several paths and certain sites can be shared by different paths. A reception after a concert for example can be visited by local and regional politicians, members of the regional arts council and their major corporate donors, therewith creating a site that brings different paths together.

K. Van Assche et al., *Evolutionary Governance Theory*, SpringerBriefs in Economics,
DOI: 10.1007/978-3-319-00984-1_4, © The Author(s) 2014

4.2 Dependencies

Actors in a governance path, in a given configuration of institutions, cannot freely change the course of governance. The path is subject to dependencies. We distinguish path dependence, interdependence and goal dependence (Shtaltovna et al. 2013; Van Assche et al. 2011).

Path dependence refers to legacies from the past that impact the course of governance (Van Assche et al. 2011; North 2005; cf. Callon 1991). The concept of path-dependence was first theorized under that name in political science in the early eighties (see North 2005 for an overview; also Eggertsson 1990, 2005; Avid 2007), while the phenomena referred to were already observed and theorized in anthropology and history (Claude Levi-Strauss, Mary Douglas, Edmund Leach, Fernand Braudel and others). Institutional economics and policy studies adopted it from political science (e.g. Ostrom 1990; North 1990; Eggertsson 1990), and more recently urban planning picked up the idea (e.g. Healey 2006).

Different definitions can be found in the literature, all referring to 'history matters', by restricting the options available in decision-making (North 2005; Whitehead 2002). Path dependencies can be manifold, and have to be distinguished empirically. Path dependencies can reside in the presence of certain actors (and their conservative views or strategies), the presence of certain formal institutions (restraining change), informal institutions (in the guise of traditions, or traditional ways to deal with formal institutions), and, in some societies, dead institutions. The latter can be described as passive path dependencies, with the capacity of dragging the path towards an older course, without being able to replicate exactly that older course. Path dependencies can also be located in a specific dialectics between formal and informal institutions, and between actors and institutions. If certain formal rules are informally linked to the identity of the community, they are likely to remain respected and guide governance in a certain direction. If a new coalition of actors enters, that same association between rule and (rejected) identity can inspire a conspicuous breaking of the rule, or a strong effort to change it. Furthermore power relations, legitimation procedures, organizational and larger cultures, as shared understandings of the situation can all be seen as legacies of the past that influence governance paths (Foucault 2003; Scott 1998).

Interdependence is in a first sense interdependence between actors in a governance process, but also the relations between the different institutions and between actors and institutions can be conceptualised as interdependencies. Each step on a governance path is conditioned, not only by the previous steps, but also by the pattern of actors and institutions that evolved over time. Once environmentalists enter local governance, the strategizing of merchants will have to take into account their presence. Besides blocking or complementing each other's strategies, actors over time can develop other roles, linked to specific contributions to accepted common goods. The local environmentalists can be a pain for the local merchants, but after a while a clean and green environment can be considered an acceptable common good by the chamber of commerce, partly because it brings in some residents and visitors, partly because it turns out less expensive than feared. The green faction in city council meetings can then be expected to play its green role by the other actors. So, interdependence is relevant for actors in strategizing towards their own goals, and in furthering common goals.

At a larger scale, the coupling between function systems adds a layer of interdependence in governance. The potential next step and the effects of that step are co-determined by the pattern of structural couplings between function systems. The relative position of each function system in a society, versus the other systems influence the way in which communications in that system gain effect in that society. In a society where the legal system is subordinate to the political system it might not be useful to resort to the courts in case certain political actors break the law in their political strategizing. If markets are very free and citizens are seen first of all as bearers of property rights, local governance will be less likely to come up with spatial plans to further certain common goods (Van Assche et al. 2013). If local laws are easily shot down by regional courts, then local governance can develop in the direction of formal passivity and increasing reliance on informal coordination.

Goal dependence, finally, is dependence on the future, or, in other terms, the influence of shared visions or plans on changes in the actor/institution configuration. Goal dependence can be linked to Aristotle's idea of the *causa finalis*, final cause. It does not mean that the future magically determines the present. Rather it implies that certain shared visions of the future and their presence in institutions, such as plans and policies, and in the discursive worlds of actors and the community at large has real effects. Explaining the evolution of actor/institution configurations in many communities is hardly possible without mentioning the influence of visions, from concrete plans to the vaguest of hopes, whether actors or communities are aware of them or not. Hopes can be interpreted as realities, visions can be confused with existing situations, what ought to be can perfuse what is. Goal dependence becomes especially relevant when politics is more than coordination, when visions of the future are formed and translated into policies.

Each governance path will be different and unique in its combination of path dependencies, interdependencies and goal dependencies. Each form of dependence can be considered an aspect of the *rigidity* of governance paths. Yet their interplay also creates *flexibility*. This can be better understood if we bring back a few notions introduced earlier. Interdependence between actors in most cases is interdependence between organizations (with individuals representing organizations), and these are not fully transparent to each other, even when there are no stratagems at play. This means that there will be a difference between actual and perceived interdependence, and between the perceptions of interdependence on different sides. Coordinated strategies acknowledging this interdependence are thus likely to produce unanticipated effects. Path dependence, is generally even more elusive for the actors themselves, as it involves images of the past, images that are necessarily constructed in the present (Teampau and Van Assche 2007). Many actors will not be aware of structural path dependencies, and if so, they will, in asserting their autonomy towards them, operate on the basis of imperfect images of self and past. Actions inspired by interpretations of path dependency are therefore likely to have unanticipated effects which, in turn, modify the pattern of path dependence. Regarding goal dependence, one can say that the unanticipated effects here are most significant, since one deals with images of futures that are utterly unknowable and steering attempts to bring that future closer that are, in a systems perspective, bound to hit the wall of other autopoietic systems, opaque and unwilling to be steered from outside. We enter the old discussion on 'implementation' here, with implementation often reduced in bureaucratic discourse to one final step of policy making or planning, while in reality, the policy or plan itself has no magical power to reshaping reality (Beunen and Duineveld 2010; Pressman and Wildavsky 1979). It only has effects insofar as existing actors incorporate it in their future interactions, which will be subjected to powers and interpretations not foreseeable in the present.

4.3 Path Creation

The way each dependency plays out in a governance situation simultaneously paves the way for its slow modification. The three dependencies interact and therewith the level of uncertainty and the importance of unanticipated consequences increases. Goal dependencies will interact with path dependencies and interdependencies. Furthering goals is only possible building on the interdependent web of actors and institutions and cannot avoid probably hardly understood path dependencies. Patterns of interdependence are affected by plans for the future and the way they affect path dependence. Path dependencies will affect the implementation of plans, yet these plans can have effects that modify the pattern of interdependence, which might resolve some aspects of path dependency. Shifts in actor/institution configurations can be explained by the interactions between the three dependencies, but not entirely. *Path creation* is possible, and is partly the result of spaces for contingency, freedom, built into the governance system. Partly it also emerges out of the interactions between the dependencies, where there are always unanticipated consequences. Understanding dependencies and path creation, rigidity and flexibility, is helpful in the understanding of steering, planning and their limitations. Actors, institutions and expertise can contribute to changes in the path, but none in separation.

This being said, interdependence does emerge as the basic condition for the reproduction of governance. Path dependence and goal dependence have to be understood against this background. It is in the necessary interplay between actors, between actors and institutions, and between formal and informal institutions, that every next step in a governance path is set, that path dependencies receive their substance, and that the visions of the future have an impact in the present.

In the next chapter, we investigate the implications of our perspective on governance paths and their dependencies for the construction of subjects and objects in governance, the inclusion of subjects and objects in policies and plans and the implementation of such new formalities.

References

Avid, A. P. (2007). Path dependence: A foundational concept for historical social science. *Cliometrica, 1*, 91–114.

Beunen, R., & Duineveld, M. (2010). Divergence and convergence in policy meanings of European environmental policies: The case of the birds and habitats directives. *International Planning Studies, 15*(1), 321–333.

Callon, M. (1991). Techno-economic networks and irreversibility. In J. Law (Ed.), *A sociology of monsters: Essays on power, technology and domination* (pp. 132–165). London: Routledge.

Eggertsson, T. (1990). *Economic behavior and institutions: Principles of neo-institutional economics*. Cambridge: Cambridge University Press.

Eggertsson, T. (2005). *Imperfect institutions: Possibilities and limits of reform*. Ann Arbor: University of Michigan Press.

Foucault, M. (2003). *Society must be defended: lectures at the College de France, 1975–76*. London: Allen Lane The Penguin Press.

Healey, P. (2006). Transforming governance: Challenges of institutional adaptation and a new politics of space. *European Planning Studies, 14*(3), 299–319.

North, D. C. (1990). *Institutions, institutional change and economic performance*. Cambridge: Cambridge University Press.

North, D. C. (2005). *Understanding the process of economic change*. Princeton: Princeton University Press.

Ostrom, E. (1990). *Governing the commons: The evolution of institutions for collective action*. Cambridge: Cambridge University Press.

Pressman, J. L., & Wildavsky, A. B. (1979). *Implementation: How great expectations in Washington are dashed in Oakland* (2d ed.). Berkeley: University of California Press.

Scott, J. C. (1998). *Seeing Like a state: How certain schemes to improve the human condition have failed*. New Haven: Yale University Press.

Shtaltovna, A., Van Assche, K., & Hornidge, A. K. (2013). Where did this debt come from? Organizational change, role ambiguity and development in rural Khorezm, Uzbekistan. *International Quarterly for Asian Studies. Internationales Asienforum 43*(3–4), 179–197.

Teampau, P., & Van Assche, K. (2007). Sulina, the dying city in a vital region. Social memory and nostalgia for the European future. *Ethnologia Balkanica, 11*(1), 257–278.

Van Assche, K., Beunen, R., Duineveld, M., & de Jong, H. (2013). Co-evolutions of planning and design: Risks and benefits of design perspectives in planning systems. *Planning Theory, 12*(2), 177–198.

Van Assche, K., Beunen, R., Jacobs, J., & Teampau, P. (2011). Crossing trails in the marshes: Rigidity and flexibility in the governance of the Danube Delta. *Journal of Environmental Planning and Management, 54*(8), 997–1018.

Van Assche, K., & Djanibekov, N. (2012). Spatial planning as policy integration: The need for an evolutionary perspective. Lessons from Uzbekistan. *Land Use Policy, 29*(1), 179–186.

Whitehead, L. (2002). *Democratization: Theory and Experience*. Oxford: Oxford Univeristy Press.

Chapter 5
Seeing, Making and Distributing Things

Abstract In this chapter we investigate the construction of subjects and objects in governance paths, the inclusion of those in policies and plans, and their impact via implementation. Implementation is understood as a process, and policies are considered temporary constructs coordinating power/knowledge, but continuously affected by other power/knowledge configurations.

5.1 Object Formation and Subject Formation

The actor/institution configurations in governance paths produce many things. First of all they produce actors and institutions (Van Assche et al. 2011; Foucault 1994). Some actors are formed in governance and others enter it. Some exist as organizations or individuals with a specific interest before any involvement in collective decision-making; others did not. Even those groups and individuals interested in certain goals and topics, cannot be considered 'actors' before inclusion in governance. Once these organizations or individuals are included as actors, they are also transformed in and through the interactions with other actors and the institutional configurations. New actors that are formed within governance can emerge in various ways: existing elements in society can be assembled around a common goal at the instigation of other actors, or in response to the actions of others. The outcomes of governance can be observed in a positive or negative way in the social environment and cause some to engage themselves in governance. The lack of certain outcomes can have the same effect. Internal discussions within actors in governance can lead to segments feeling alienated and either withdrawing from participation within the actor (thus further changing it) or to segments becoming involved separately, therewith creating a new actor (Van Assche 2007; Van Assche et al. 2012).

The productivity of governance is more substantial than the creation of actors. Governance creates both subjects and objects (Van Assche et al. 2011; Duineveld and Van Assche 2011; Duineveld et al. 2013). The production and transformation

K. Van Assche et al., *Evolutionary Governance Theory*, SpringerBriefs in Economics, DOI: 10.1007/978-3-319-00984-1_5,

of actors in governance are processes of subject formation that along with the production of new identities, produces new subjectivities and new visions of the world. The perspective on object and subject creation allows us to see more of the discursive mechanics at play within governance evolutions and it allows us to map more of the routes in which discursive worlds seep into the continuously transforming game. This perspective is inspired by both the early and the late works of Michel Foucault (Foucault 1966, 1972, 1980, 1998, 2006).

If we see actors as subjects that are transformed in governance, then it is easier to grasp the many potential links with visions of the world, of desirable and less desirable futures. In most cases actors are groups, or individuals or organizations representing groups. These actors define themselves by reference to goals, but usually these actors have implied ideas about the existing, feared and desired worlds, of the past, present and future (Van Assche et al. 2012). If these actors are clearly defined, and equipped with fully developed narratives before entering governance, this might give these narratives more impact on governance, without however avoiding an influence of governance on these narratives themselves. If they are weakly or partially developed, there is a bigger chance that the governance experience itself will lead to further development of the discursive equipment of the actor. In governance, a green party cannot remain green, it has to develop ideas on other aspects of the world, and the new positions of the green party are likely to represent identity politics within the governance process (the green party might highlight their difference from party X and their similarity to party Y).

Exposure to governance can also lead, maybe more concretely, to the embracing of objects as important by certain subjectivities. Subjectivities, as constructed identities, can associate themselves with certain objects, in such a way that the involvement and/or the object becomes part of the identity, of the subjectivity (Delanty 2003). One can think of European green parties in the seventies and trees or American neo- conservatives and guns. Objects can be (concepts of) physical objects, such as trees and guns, but also places, groups, issues and topics, or abstract concepts and the embedding ideologies. Some of these objects are the product of governance itself, other enter it and are transformed within governance.

Both objects and subjects are the product of discursive evolutions and governance is a realm of high discursive productivity: new actors are formed in the process; others are entering it and are being redefined. The objects they are dealing with might come in and be altered, or they are the product of the process itself. Governance can create new associations between objects and subjects, in some cases redefining subjectivity.

In keeping with the terminology presented in previous chapters, we distinguish between paths, sites, and mechanisms of object and subject formation (Duineveld and Van Assche 2011; Duineveld et al. 2013). Not every path of object and subject formation is on the terrain of governance, but governance sites are certainly sites of object and subject formation. With their continuous confrontation between versions of the world and the pressure exerted on discursively by the need to take decisions, governance paths are highly productive series of sites. Mechanisms (or techniques) are sometimes applied consciously, strategically (as part of stratagems) by actors, but in many cases they occur unintentionally and invisibly, as a result of interactions between actors and evolving actor/institution configurations. After two weeks of negotiations about a new cabinet, each party is a little different, and for each of them, several objects will be new or newly important.

In the techniques of object formation, we distinguish between reification, solidification and codification (Duineveld et al. 2013). Reification entails the recognition of the object as a unity, separated from its environment, more than a loose assemblage of parts. A tree becomes visible, rather than branches and leafs; a forest becomes visible, rather than a collection of trees. Solidification refers to the tightening of internal connections in the concept, an increasingly sharp delineation of the emerging discursive object. Branches and leafs are recognized as elements of a tree, as linked and necessary parts, and probably requiring a root. Codification is the simplification of the object boundaries. It comes with the simple applicability of codes to decide on conceptual inclusion/exclusion. The bird on the branch and the worm on the leaf are not considered part of the tree, the wanderer in the forest becomes a matter of discussion.

As a second, sometimes separate, sometimes less discernible stage of object formation, we can speak of object stabilization. As techniques of object stabilization, we distinguish objectification, naturalization, and institutionalization. Naturalization is the strengthening of the public perception that the object is part of the order of things, part of nature. It is the process that veils contingency, blinds the awareness that things could have been different, that objects could have been constructed differently (Latour and Woolgar 1986). 'Of course this is the forest? What else could it be?' -sacred grove, dark place, tree plantation, place of chaos and wildness, hunting ground. Naturalization is creation of the aura of the obvious, the incorporation of the object into the warehouse of unquestioned commonplaces. With that, the policy implications of the new object tend to sneak in public awareness, tend to become more easily acceptable. If forests are ecosystems and ecosystems are fragile, important and useful, then protection might seem appropriate; if forests are plantations, then management is a matter of cutting and planting.

Objectification completes the process of reification. Objectification, then, is the acknowledgment of the object as part of the objective truth, established by scientific means (Latour and Woolgar 1986). Especially in administrations or other governance arena's where scientific expertise is expected to reduce the burden of political decision- making, this step can increase the impact of the object on governance. If some birds are seen in the bulb fields, they can become assembled into the new object of 'bulb birds', and once scientists study and count the bulb birds, this assemblage becomes an objective unity that can fare well or not so well (Duineveld and Van Assche 2011). Institutionalization is the codification of discourse, including its objects, in organizations, policies and plans. If the bulb birds are recognized and doing not so well, they can be protected, the planning of bulb areas can be altered, and maybe no residential development should take place in these fragile ecosystems. One can notice here a metaphoric slide: the new object can shift the meaning of its environment, which in turn can have new policy implications.

In governance, no construct is entirely stable (Duineveld et al. 2013; cf. Mol 2002). The techniques of object stabilization are never perfect and always likely to encounter strategies pushing for moulding or deconstruction of the object. In other words, the construction of irreversibility is never perfect. The radically constructed nature of subject and object does not deny the agency or the constraining role of the material environment in the process of object formation (Duineveld and Van Assche 2011). Neither does it contradict the role of human agency. What does transpire in our perspective is that in evolving governance both objects and subjects are transformed, that this is partly a matter of strategy, and partly a matter of discursive evolution outside the control and/or the view of the participants. Actor/institution configurations produce effects anticipated by no one, and these effects include object formation. The reproduction of the actor/institution configuration is driven by actions, and these actions are structured by discursive worlds partly produced in governance.

5.2 Boundaries

If governance evolution is discursively productive, this can be analysed as the production of objects and subjects, whereby mechanisms of formation can be distinguished. At a more elementary level, we can study the construction of boundaries underlying object and subject construction. Analysing boundary formation, maintenance and change can shed a different light on the relations between objects and subjects, and on other relations in governance.

Since our epistemology is constructivist, a constructivism that accounts for materiality, agency and the agency of materiality, we start with the discursive construction of reality, and then we reincorporate the non-discursive. That means that we preliminarily consider all boundaries *conceptual boundaries. Spatial boundaries and social boundaries*, delineating respectively places and social identities, are considered special categories of conceptual boundaries (Van Assche et al. 2008). Conceptual boundaries delineate objects and subjects (social identities), and they delineate places. The process of delineation can start from the interior and from the exterior, i.e. it can start with the demarcation of a difference, and it can start with the crystallization of relations, which then become considered as interior, and delineated. One can define one tree as first of all different from the next one, or from a different species, and one can come to the concept of tree by means of gradual observation of the relations between roots, branches and leafs. Possibly the root becomes part of the tree later, as an externally delineated addition of something that emerged as a set of internal relations.

Not all conceptual boundaries are spatial or social, as not all discursive objects are places or subjects, so we call the rest, for simplicity's sake, conceptual boundary. Conceptual, social and spatial boundaries entangle, and, as with metaphors, their similarity as boundaries enables the carry- over of other meanings. Since all are in essence discursive constructions, they are more related than it seems, than one tends to think after the processes of codification, naturalization, et cetera we discussed earlier. This means that they can entangle more easily than people usually think. Meanings can be carried over more easily from one object to another, and redrawing one boundary, or creating new associations between objects, tends to spark off effects in boundary construction, hence object construction.

Spatial boundaries can be the result of existing social boundaries and they can trigger new social boundaries. They can also trigger the formation of new conceptual boundaries, or objects, with which social groups can identify. Whereas social boundaries can emerge from spatial boundaries, from contrast with other social identities, from association with material objects or practices, they can also produce new associations with objects, subjects and spaces (Van Assche et al. 2008; Elias and Scotson 1994). An ethnic group can recognize itself as group only when confronted with others behaving differently; the teapot that was just a teapot can become distinctive, and other groups can start producing teapots that are purposefully different. The people from an area in Western Europe can be Celts, and when the area becomes France, and France becomes more unified and recognized, these people might become the French. They can morph into French as a result of policies fostering identification, as a result of slow identification by many small communities, or because all foreigners and some local groups (becoming 'minorities') call them French. The identification might be fostered by a political centre, or it might be actively promoted (and reconstructed) at the edge, in a border zone where spatial and social boundaries are disputed.

A special category of conceptual objects that shape boundaries in governance evolution, we call *images of history*, or historical narratives. History can give depth to objects and subjects, can harden their boundaries, intensify the process of object stabilization, and render them more a part of the natural order. 'It was always like this'. In terms of subjects, if these subjects are or become actors in governance, then the use of history and the reconstruction of history in governance can intensify or smoothen oppositions between actors. History can focus the strategizing of the actors, by clarifying identity, but it can also reduce governance to identity politics and block attempts at mutual understanding or reflexivity. All these efforts can look useless if the actors start from the assumption that they know perfectly well what they are and what they want, and that historical depth and continuity is the proof of their conviction. 'This is what we stand for because this is what we are and we are what we are because we have been like this forever'. Images of history thus permit tautologies that render reflexivity harder, that make it harder to redraw object and subject boundaries in governance, a redrawing that is part and parcel of the negotiations of democratic governance. Images of history can thus be said to *harden the boundaries of the actors*, which makes governance less flexible and adaptive.

Similarly, history, i.e. images of history as conceptual objects, can *harden spatial boundaries*. In the case of spatial boundaries, institutionalization in administrative and political structures (municipalities, watershed commissions, regional governments) often combines with images of history to produce hard spatial boundaries that are not reflected upon anymore. Many issues of course do not respect these spatial boundaries, and many of these boundaries could also be constructed and considered differently, even if only in the context of deliberation.

Also in devising appropriate policies and in assessing the impact of policies, the hardening of spatial boundaries as a result of images of history and institutionalization, the associated forgetting of the contingent character, and permeability of these spatial boundaries can become problematic. We can speak, with Bruno Latour, of *blackboxing* of objects after hardening of boundaries (Latour 1999). Policies, embedded goals, or (spatial) impacts of policies are often considered, their results measured against the background of a landscape that is presumed neutral, where the contingent character of spatial boundaries, and the entanglement with the other boundaries, is black boxed. Both material flows and discursive flows do not respect these boundaries, but if hard enough, this is forgotten. And such forgetting means that potentially superior policies become invisible. If an urban area is, for historical reasons, perceived and organized as a collection of 17 villages, then traffic flows, commercial development and green infrastructure will probably not be managed and planned well, and investment in heritage, preservation and redevelopment will not be directed in the most efficient and most beneficial manner.

All this being said, the material world does assert itself in boundary construction. It is just that we are never sure how and when (cf. Eco 2000; Bryant 2011). Watersheds, ecosystems, certain landscape types (think marshes, mountains, and deserts) have boundaries that have effects on discursive construction and human actions, on discursive and material flows. Man-made landscapes (think cities, mining landscapes, industrial wastelands, and polluted areas, but also parks, high quality neighbourhoods) can have similar effects; they can affect the formation of spatial, social, and other conceptual boundaries. Poor people can end up in marshes, or in polluted areas, but marshes can also attract affluent birdwatchers, who over time can built their own colony next to the Heron's colony.

For people however (and for social systems), it is not possible to distinguish between the physical environment and discursive environment. All meaning, whether psychic or social, depends on an internal construction of the outside world, the environment. We cannot operative beyond our discursive worlds, and even if we can certainly hit a wall in that landscape, and can see that many birds hit that wall, the birds, the wall, the landscape, and the series of relations and inferences associated with the designation of the wall as boundary, are all discursively delineated. One of the consequences is that one *cannot distinguish between the physical environment as obstacle (therefore boundary) and the effects of previous discursive activity that hardened into obstacles*. It cannot tell the difference between physical boundaries and the results of the activities of social systems (and psychic systems).

For that reason, we speak of *empirical boundaries*, as boundaries that function as boundaries but do not originate in the internal semantics of the observing subject or system. Some of these boundaries are associated with natural physical obstacles and ecosystem boundaries; others are forgotten effects of human activity or effects of forgotten human activity. The activities, sometimes the effects, were once present in and structured by discursive worlds, but they are forgotten, disappeared from discourse, or *externalized.* These externalizations can come back to haunt us, and appear as natural obstacles, as physical boundaries later. Environmental pollution e.g. can be unobserved for a long time, while forming an obstacle for many human activities; it can create spatial boundaries of which the origin is not always reflected upon. Forests can be cleared a long time ago, and the ecological consequences account for a landscape that imposes its boundaries on many human activities (and understandings). In other words, a community experiences an obstacle, that obstacle is perceived as a physical, natural boundary, but one can never tell for sure what the origin of the obstacle is, and, related, what the precise influence of the material difference was on the construction of differences (hence objects and boundaries) in discourse (cf. Eco 2000).

These resonances between various sorts of boundaries are relevant to governance, because actors are discursively bounded subjects, in the sense of individuals (a product of narration) and in the sense of social identities, operating on the basis of social boundaries. Because governance in most cases is governance of a place or territory, delineated by spatial boundaries, collective decision-making involves other spatial and social objects too. Decision-making is about something, places, topics, issues, and all these receive their discursive identity because of conceptual boundaries that are likely to be transformed in the process of governance. Spatial, social and chronological boundaries (places, subjects and images of history) can harden a path of governance when they are not disputed. They can also make the path more unpredictable and the process more volatile when they are disputed, reducing governance to identity politics.

5.3 Policy, Knowledge/Power, and Implementation

In evolving governance, many things happen. Objects and subjects are under constant pressure of redefinition, formal and informal institutions co-evolve, while actors and institutions do the same. At this point in the reasoning, it is necessary to address two more essential concepts: knowledge and power. *Power* we define, in line with Foucault, as a set of immanent force relations that is present and working everywhere and in every direction (Foucault 1998). Power is neither good nor bad, it is not necessarily tied to individual or group action, desire, and intentionality. Rather, it is the web of forces at micro- level that make things at the same time possible and understandable and that allows for aggregations of power at higher levels of understanding and authority. Power and knowledge are thus entwined (Flyvbjerg 1998). In governance, where collectively binding decisions are strived for, and decisions with an impact on the lives of many are institutionalised (e.g. in the form of policies, plans, and laws), this is all the more true.

In the governance process, power and knowledge are always entwined. Knowledge independent of the web of power relations that produced it, does not exist, and vice versa, power independent of a version of the world that is promoted, does not exist. *Knowledge*, then, is the insight made possible by others insights and the way they interweave with power. It is not restricted to scientific knowledge, while conversely, no special epistemological status is assigned to 'local knowledge' (Fischer 2000). Local knowledge, scientific knowledge, and the more clearly politicized forms of knowledge present in reports for and by administrations, are all entwined with power. None of them can claim to a direct access to the truth, and none of them can be decoupled from power relations. This can be understood at several levels: no form of knowledge can be fully dis-embedded from organizations, from communities, groups, or from a set of topics, methods and questions that structures the production of each form of knowledge. These observations lead to the double assertion already made: direct access to reality, to truth, does not exist, and embedding in communities, thus power relations, cannot be avoided.

Governance, as we know, both serves and creates actors and objects. It also leads to decisions which can be codified in policies, plans, and laws. Policies we consider the standard codification here, with plans representing a second codification, and laws a reinterpretation into the function system of law (Luhmann 2004). We can discern another angle to look at governance now. Governance is continuously shifting networks of governmental and non- governmental agents, it is strategizing with power/knowledge, and it is the production of policies. Actors can utilize knowledge to reinforce their own position of power, while delegitimizing the knowledge of competing actors. Directly or indirectly, this can dis-enfranchises knowledge held dear by citizens, and the citizens themselves. Representation of citizens is representation of understandings of the world, and also in this sense, power/knowledge configurations cannot be extricated.

If we understand, with Foucault, knowledge as discursively produced in discourses that evolve, compete, and transform, and that both open and close reality for us because of the necessity of simplifications, then we can present governance also as a continuous battle over the simplifications, reductions of complexity, or models of the world that will exert more influence over the future community. Each discourse, each perspective on a part of reality creates that reality for us. Yet, the choices implied for one or another construction simultaneously veil alternative constructions, alternative delineations of objects and subjects, backgrounds and relations. Governance deploys and produces discourse and can therefore create and uphold social realities, while making alternatives less visible and less likely to happen. Governance is a process in which discourses compete and transform, partly as a result of stratagems by actors, partly because of the process itself, the unique reproductive logic of the reigning actor/institution configuration. Governance paths are therefore paved with sites of conflict, open and latent, in which power/knowledge are transformed more intensely in and by the conflict. Power conflicts give rise to conflicting versions of reality and different versions of reality, past, present or future can trigger power conflicts. Policies, as results of governance, can solve conflicts, freeze them, and produce new ones.

Policies appear now as a tool of coordination of governmental and non- governmental actors, not only as a supposed final result of coordination. Governance never stops, and governance as an on-going competition between discourses never leads to a unifying discourse that fully represents the community and is capable of addressing its key issues in manners acceptable to all. Policies appear as temporary conceptual structures coordinating knowledge and power, in constant transmutation, because of the confrontations with other power/knowledge configurations.

This view is useful to study the vagaries of policies, from emergence to application: how do various arenas of power/knowledge, at several scales, crystallize policies that consequently impact those arenas? Policies entering one arena are reinterpreted and used differently, even by the same actor, in different arena's, and at different stages. Policies are always and everywhere opposed, ignored, reinterpreted, repackaged, forgotten, and selectively enforced or implemented, because each arena, and each moment in an arena, represents a different power/knowledge environment, a different set of oppositions and transformation options. '*Implementation*' of policies is therefore a process of continuous reinterpretation, of divergence and convergence, of adaptation to new power/knowledge configurations in new discursive environments, to new objects and subjects, and to new coordinative rules (institutions) (Beunen and Duineveld 2010).

These insights add to the understanding of uncertainty and unpredictability in governance. They also expose rhetoric of stability, consensus, uniformity, and shared values and goals as not only difficult to achieve, but also to what it is: rhetoric, which can be used and abused in the on-going confrontations in governance. The same applies to notions of transparency and truth. Science, as knowledge promising more direct access to reality, and more direct answers to objective issues existing in society and supposedly asking for answers, is therefore exceedingly prone to use and abuse in governance. It's used to solve problems that cannot be solved, to answer questions that do not have an answer, or to reduce and replace thorny social issues with manageable yet different issues.

To get a better grasp on the issue of expertise and its promises in governance, the next chapter takes a closer look at the power of stories.

References

Beunen, R., & Duineveld, M. (2010). Divergence and convergence in policy meanings of European environmental policies: the case of the birds and habitats directives. *International Planning Studies, 15*(1), 321–333.

Bryant, L. R. (2011). *The democracy of objects*. Michigan: Open Humanities Press.

Delanty, G. (2003). *Community*. London: Routledge.

Duineveld, M., & Van Assche, K. (2011). The power of tulips: constructing nature and heritage in a contested landscape. *Journal of Environmental Policy and Planning, 13*(2), 1–20.

Duineveld, M., Van Assche, K., & Beunen, R. (2013). Making things irreversible. Object stabilization in urban planning and design. *Geoforum, 46*, 16–24.

Eco, U. (2000). *Kant and the platypus: Essays on language and cognition*. New York: Harcourt Brace.

Elias, N., & Scotson, J. L. (1994). *The established and the outsiders: A sociological enquiry into community problems*. London: Sage.

Fischer, F. (2000). *Citizens, experts and the environment. The politics of local knowledge.* Durham: Duke University Press.
Flyvbjerg, B. (1998). *Rationality and power: Democracy in practice.* Chicago: University of Chicago Press.
Foucault, M. (1966). *Les mots et les choses.* Parijs: Gallimard.
Foucault, M. (1972). *The archaeology of knowledge and the discourse on language.* New York: Pantheon Books.
Foucault, M. (1980). *Power/knowledge: Selected interviews and other writings, 1972–1977.* New York: Pantheon Books.
Foucault, M. (1994). The subject and power. In J. D. Faubion (Ed.), *Power. Essential works of foucault 1954–1984. Volume 3.* New York: The new press.
Foucault, M. (1998). *The will to knowledge. The history of sexuality: 1.* London: Penguin Books.
Foucault, M. (2006). *History of madness.* London and New York: Routledge.
Latour, B. (1999). *Pandora's hope: Essays on the reality of science studies.* London: Harvard University Press.
Latour, B., & Woolgar, S. (1986). *Laboratory life: The construction of scientific facts.* Princeton, N.J.: Princeton University Press.
Luhmann, N. (2004). *Law as a social system.* Oxford: Oxford University Press.
Mol, A. (2002). *The body multiple: Ontology in medical practice.* Durham: Duke University Press.
Van Assche, K., & 1. (2007). Planning as/and/in context. Towards a new analysis of participatory planning. *METU JFA, 27*(1), 110–119.
Van Assche, K., Bell, S., & Teampau, P. (2012). Traumatic natures in the swamp. Concepts of nature and participatory governance in the Danube delta. *Environmental Values, 21*(2), 163–183.
Van Assche, K., Duineveld, M., Beunen, R., & Teampau, P. (2011). Delineating locals: Transformations of knowledge/power and the governance of the Danube delta. *Journal of Environmental Policy and Planning, 13*(1), 1–21.
Van Assche, K., Teampau, P., Devlieger, P., & Sucio, C. (2008). Liquid boundaries in marginal marshes. Reconstructions of identity in the romanian Danube delta. *Studia Sociologia, 39*(1), 115–138.

Chapter 6
The Power of Stories

Abstract In this chapter we discuss a special form of discursive structure, narrative, and its effects. Metaphors and open concepts are analysed as concepts that have effects amplified in narratives. These effects can vary from closing the narrative to opening it, from linking by suggesting similarity to disconnecting by suggesting dissimilarity. Ideologies are then presented as embedding narratives.

6.1 Narratives

What often gives objects, actors and institutions more stability and power, is their embedding in narratives, which can in turn be embedded in ideologies (Zizek 1989). Narratives provide frames to interpret situations, they can link objects, actors and institutions in preferable or understandable manners, and they can produce objects, actors and institutions (Abu-Lughod 1992; Bal 1985; Sandercock 2003).

A narrative is a conceptual structure that can render discursive materials more real and more compelling by introducing temporal, spatial and emotional order (Czarniawska 1998). It is an assemblage of concepts, subjects, objects and events. It articulates, criteria and values, events and episodes, flights and climaxes, heroes and villains, foreground and background. In line with Levi- Strauss, we say that it is the structure of the narrative that has the effects (Lévi-Strauss 1968). What narratives share is that structure, and this is what apparently explains the similar effects narratives can have in terms of emotional grip, reality effects, and entertainment. It is the structure that distinguishes it from other forms of discourse. Narrative form can be found and used in any aspect of social life, including law, science and economy (Austin 1962; Czarniawska 1998; Gabriel 2000; Mackenzie et al. 2007). Either discourse there itself takes on narrative form, or it assumes other narratives or incorporates concepts that derive their meaning from narratives.

Narratives are discursive structures consisting of other discursive structures and embedded in others. They have a stabilizing effect by applying structure to

K. Van Assche et al., *Evolutionary Governance Theory*, SpringerBriefs in Economics,
DOI: 10.1007/978-3-319-00984-1_6, © The Author(s) 2014

materials otherwise less interesting and less easy to grasp and convey. They consist of actors that do things, operating in a world consisting of things. A narrative is embedded in a continuously shifting discursive environment, and this is affecting its content, structure and effect. In this discursive environment, it can link or not with values, criteria, concepts characters and events in figuring in other discourses/narratives. The potential for a certain narrative to become widely accepted, shared and spread in a community depends on the structure of this discursive environment (Van Assche et al. 2012). The environment represents the potential of transformation of the narratives through the formation of discourse coalitions, coalitions of actors that share a similar discourses or narrative, that re-assemble and re- appropriate narratives or narrative fragments (cf. Hajer 1995).

The attraction of narratives as persuasive models of explanation makes them more likely to travel between governance contexts than other discursive structures. The traveling can be done as a whole or in fragments of structure, content or a combination of both. One can say that narratives invite and encourage *discursive migration* (Kooij et al. 2013). The presence of narratives in a discursive environment makes it likely that the modes of seeing and understanding embodied in the narrative move to other domains of discourse, to other topics, genres, function systems, organizations, groups and places. The stabilizing effect of a certain narrative, naturally tends to de-stabilize its environment, where other interpretive schemes can be affected by the success of this narrative. As falling domino blocks, successful narratives can alter a whole discursive landscape (Beunen et al. 2013; Rap 2006; Van Assche et al. 2012).

Narratives of self and group, of group and place, of place and history are interwoven (Van Assche et al. 2008). They are interwoven in manners that recall the discussion on boundaries and the construction of objects, subjects, places and times. Individual identity can be considered a narration and re- narration of life history, a history including other people, places and events (Elias and Scotson 1994; Elliot and Du Gay 2009; Seidl 2005; Van Assche et al. 2009). Beyond such narrative, we elude ourselves, and simple self- descriptions can be understood as stabilizing fictions rooted in more complex narratives involving history and environment. People do belong to various groups and narratives of self and group therefore entwine in intricate ways. Sometimes individuals are subsumed by groups, by one group, but in most cases, narratives of identity derived from membership serve only certain occasions and certain function in psychological and social life (Elliot and Du Gay 2009; Delanty 2003). Certain tropes, figures of style, topoi and commonplaces, can signal membership, can function as signs of social identities and their importance under certain conditions.

With all this mutual constituting going on, one should not expect that the narrative constructions of self, group, place and time are seamless or that they can be added up to a cohesive semantic universe. On the contrary, the psychological order itself is a whirlpool of competing narratives and loose discursive materials that is only apparently stabilized, and largely thanks to a social order. Narratives of self indeed serve certain functions, but these functions are not always clear to, not always understood by the individual. They do not simply exist next to each other, in a neat row of functions together making up a balanced and healthy life. Secondly, the gap between psychological and social order will alter in shape and depth all the time and can never be filled in or fixed completely by narrative means. If one can spend more time with people, one can observe that the cracks between individual and group are always there, that narratives on self never coincide with narratives of groups (or places as communities), even when references to groups and places are abundant in the self- description. Narratives can be used to create cohesion in segments of the internal and external world, and they can be used to render invisible the gaps, cracks and disjunctures always present in the collage of segments.

In governance, narratives can thus expected to be prevalent and serve many purposes. Around the metaphorical table are individuals representing interests, topics, organizations, groups, and themselves. Understanding them as actors or stakeholders representing something or someone, is certainly productive for a theory of governance, but one cannot forget that these descriptions rest on narrative schemes that have impact on observers and participants. One cannot forget that everyone around the table makes sense of herself, of the others, of the governance situation, of topics, objects and subjects in terms of narratives (Van Assche et al. 2011). Stakeholders never truly know what is at stake. Stakeholders never truly know what is their angle and who they are representing, and citizens outside the governance situation, who are not designated as 'actors', can never know if, how, in which respect, with reference to which identity they are represented. They will never know which of their incompatible narratives leads a life in collective decision- making and they will never know how they are narratively transformed by the ones 'representing' them and in the dialectical maelstrom of governance games.

In keeping with our earlier analyses of governance and discursivity, we now add that governance paths connect sites of narration, of narrative reconstruction, and of discursive migration and transformation. In governance, new narratives are produced, consciously and unconsciously, in adaptation to each other. Understandings of self, group, others and world are almost certainly transforming in the pressure cooker of governance, where confrontation with other understandings cannot be avoided and where what is persuasive can be experienced and observed directly (Van Assche et al. 2011).

In governance, it is also likely that several levels of nested narrative or several layers of discursive context, are at stake. These levels affect each other, as their boundaries are also constructed in the narratives, in the discursive context, and they are permeable. Stories about the past influence the present, stories about politics in general affect the image of the correct handling of issues in this specific governance situation, larger issues determine the perspective on smaller issues, but also the other way around. The discursive boundaries around certain objects, subjects or issues can be harder than for others, and the same is true for scales or levels. Certain narratives on the good life are more open to change from below, from series of examples or real life situation, whereas others harden themselves by explaining away the details of what can be observed as trivial. The structure and content of narratives thus affects the hardness of boundaries and therewith the potential for discursive migration, for the moving, sharing and transformation of understandings that can accompany it.

6.2 Metaphors and Open Concepts

Narratives are conceptual structures that amplify the impact of its elements, as structures that can engender discursive migration and shared understanding. Within governance particular attention should be paid to two special types of concepts: metaphors and open concepts (Bal 2002; Barnes and Duncan 1992; Eco 1976; Kooij et al. 2013; Beunen and Hagens 2009). These concepts can amplify effects and enable migration. Their own effects can be amplified by use in narratives, and they can migrate themselves, making things look more similar or more different than before, introducing new sets of similarities and differences and changing perception and valuation accordingly. Just as the narratives can be embedded in other narratives, open concepts and metaphors can be embedded in other open concepts and metaphors. For the case of metaphors, we will speak, in line with George Lakoff and Mark Johnson, of *nested metaphors and root metaphors* (Lakoff and Johnson 1980).

In ancient rhetoric, *metaphors* were presented often simply as comparisons where the 'as if' is dropped (Aristotle 1954; Aristotle and Lucas 1972). Society is a body, a family is a ship. Some of the Greek and Roman authors already perceived that metaphors allow a shift in perspective. They enable perceiving new features of an object, a person, or a situation and a new connection between these features, a new unity of the object. We can speak of a transformation of the object, a redrawing of the boundaries. Once a metaphor is adopted and spreads in a community, it tends to be stretched up. The brain is a computer, the mind is a computer, the body is a computer, organizations are computers and society as a whole might be a computer. With the over-application of the metaphor, the underlying comparison become weaker and weaker, and the shift in perspective minimalizes. Few new features are discovered, and the fact of prevalence itself makes it less likely that a new application of the prevalent metaphor will open the eyes of many.

Metaphors can have offspring. They can engender new metaphors. Once a family is a ship, the dad or mom can be the captain, financial problems can be a storm, and lower taxes can be a windfall. If a brain is a computer then the eyes are visual sensors and the visual centre is a video- card. This reproductive faculty of metaphors can lead to nested metaphors. The nesting can have other sources however. It is possible that several existing metaphors become compatible in the production of a new perspective. A community can be a beehive, its members bees playing a role, but the beehive can also be in a forest and the world can be a forest, life finding a way in, carving a habitable niche in, the forest. Societies can be marked deeply and thoroughly by root metaphors, metaphors with a remarkable longevity, a high level of abstraction, and a high level of compatibility with many other metaphors. Metaphoric concepts of man, society, God, knowledge, truth and value are prone to becoming root metaphors. They are powerful because unexamined, and because of their permeation of many discursive worlds by means of compatible metaphors. This understanding of root metaphors comes close to what Foucault called an *episteme*, a manner of knowing, a set of interpretive schemes that marks an era and a civilization (Foucault 1973). It makes a difference whether man is God, the slave of God, similar to God, or whether God is a mystery to man, especially in communities where religion is important, where functional differentiation has not fully developed, and where God is important in the organization of life, knowledge and politics.

Metaphors are devices that can link different discursive fields, and make the interpretive schemes of one field available and useful for the other one. This can generate discursive shifts in one field, the starting point of the comparison ('society is…') and it can shed a simultaneously a new light, because of the connection, on the other side of the implied comparison ('… a beehive'). The metaphor of society as beehive can refocus attention and change understanding of both the beehive and society. As always in discursive activity, subjects are entwined with objects. A new entwining of objects by means of metaphor can never be fully mapped because the subject, acquiring a new understanding of objects, cannot remove itself from the equation, cannot deduce itself simply from the new entwining, assuming that nothing changed on the subject side. The new link forged between distinct discursive fields can restructure these fields in different ways. New accents in a largely unchanged object can be placed, e.g. by emphasizing the inescapable character of roles in society. New blind spots are simultaneously introduced (the beehive makes one forget that people can change roles, or mess up a function). The metaphor can cause new associations with other objects, new assemblages, and the newly perceived unity of these can supersede the older object boundaries. Whole objects can be forgotten in this way. They can be erased by changing the internal structure of larger objects. If a family is an organization instead of a ship, it is easy to forget the wind and the storm and the impossibility to control the elements. If a person is a bee and society a beehive, then it is easy to forget the character of persons, which might have been highlighted in older sets of metaphors -man is an animal, this one a wolf, that one a sheep, another an ant. If the brains are a computer, and the mind can be reduced to the brain, then this metaphorical development has probably been prepared by a series of broader metaphorical shifts, allowing us to disconnect man from community, from God, and body from soul -to forget all these connections, and concomitantly, to forget the idea of soul and the idea of God, communicating to our souls.

Since metaphors are producing new insights by connecting semantic fields, they can have governance effects. If metaphors change, are used, connect with other metaphors, produce new metaphors, objects can form and disappear, boundaries can be redrawn, narratives can lose or gain persuasiveness, new narratives can be crafted -starting from the new metaphors and the perspective they generate. The set of discursive changes induced by changes in metaphorical activity is called a *metaphoric slide*. A metaphorical slide can amplify the effects of narratives, or it can make them lose their lustre. It can open existing concepts and narratives for re- examination and allow them to play new roles in policy discussions. It can also close them, sealing hitherto existing cracks in the boundary, rendering them less open to interpretation. Regarding the interpretation of roles in society: if society was a body where all need each other, and the village a big family, then it is a duty to help each other, but there is still much freedom of choice. If body and family are replaced by a single metaphor of beehive, the more mechanistic model ignores free will and freedom. New metaphors bring new interpretive schemes to governance, new sets of similarities and dissimilarities within and between objects. New similarities can forge new discursive connections, new dissimilarities can break them, and new patterns of (dis)similarities have their own higher order effects on making and breaking discursive bonds. A different colour might make something not a strawberry, while colour plus shape plus taste might make it a new type of pomegranate.

Such restructuring of (dis)similarity can also be observed with a second special type of concepts, *open concepts* (Kooij et al. 2013; Gunder and Hillier 2010). They too, can be embedded in narrative, be amplified in their effects by narratives, and travel with narrative. They too, have their own tendency to migrate, and to shift discursive configurations in faraway places. Yet, other than metaphors, open concepts do not produce perspectival shifts and object transformation because of imported interpretive schemes or because of new structures. Rather, they break open the local discursive structure with an emptiness that invites continuous reinterpretation. Open concepts are seemingly vague concepts that play nevertheless crucial roles in the reproduction of governance, one could think of concepts such as sustainability, spatial quality, identity, creative economies and innovation. Often, scientists and governance actors alike complain about that vague character, not recognizing the importance of the openness. At the same time, the impression of precision cannot only undermine the positive functions of open concepts; it can also veil the openness and allow it to function unexamined. What are those positive functions?

At a first level, seeming emptiness is also fullness. Just as a vague poem can mean many things, an extremely vague poem very many things and a white sheet of poetry paper everything. So vague concepts mean ever more when they get vaguer and potentially everything when they are empty. The limit of discursive fullness is thus emptiness, an emptiness where presence and absence paradoxically coexist. Sustainability for example, can mean many things; the absence of precise discursive articulation enables the coexistence of many different meanings (Gunder and Hillier 2010). Such coexistence has many advantages in governance situations: one can pick and choose, one can pretend to agree while each picking a different meaning, and one can keep the discussion going by hiding behind the open concept, by glossing over differences, avoiding hard confrontations and maybe the grinding halt of governance. This buys time and preserves social and political capital. Over time power/knowledge configurations might shift and unlock the situation. Open concepts migrate easily, since they can accommodate the hybridization and transformation caused by travel well (Bal 2002). But they also play the role of pinning down knots of discourses which tend to move in different directions. In Lacanian terms, one can speak of a *point de capiton* (Lacan 1977). A new school with green roof, a shallower ditch, more trees, a story on local creative economies, a story of support for local farmers, a story on maintaining community identity, all can huddle together for specific purposes (a project, a policy) under the flag of sustainability. The pinning down, the precision of it, has to be partly fictitious to remain functional. The appearance of precision (hence discursive closure) has to be de facto discursive openness. The arrogant architect, for example, asserts that 'nobody needs to tell him what quality architecture is'; he recognizes it when he sees it. He probably changed his idea on quality architecture hundreds of times in his career, but his arrogance, the impression of certainty and precision hide an openness that allows the practical process of design and development to continue.

Open concepts *can* but not necessarily do play the role of *master signifier*, as a signifier of a totality, a wholeness and completeness that cannot exist in reality, but is nevertheless desirable (Stavrakakis 1999). This for example becomes visible in the narrative about the new building proposed by the architect that will strengthen local spatial identity and restore community spirit and unity. While a unified community is necessarily a fiction, and a stable and single spatial identity, linked to such fictitious community is just as impossible. Yet each of the invoked fictions is productive. 'Community' can be considered the master signifier, the grounding trope of a desired unity in the social body, which has to ground every aspect of governance. Striving for community has effects; the presence of the master signifier in governance can bring about a striving for consensus that would otherwise not exist. It can make policies and plans more realistic, but it can also, if the hopes are too high, make real bumps on the road to policy implementation invisible, as it can ignore real cleavages in the community that have to be acknowledged and dealt with in the open.

So open concepts serve as a crystallization point of various discourses and enabler of their reproduction (Asimakou 2009; Gunder and Hillier 2010; Jeffares 2007). Since governance paths and sites are par eminence occasions where discourses meet, compete and have to come to accommodations, open concepts are likely to play an important role there. They can function as a middle ground where consensus can be achieved or pretended, where goals can be mentioned but suspended. Governance deals with small and big issues in a context that politicizes them and that can transform them by seeing them in the light of grander narratives and their differences. Within such situation open concepts can enter their role of master signifier easily. A discussion on school lunches can end up in a discussion on the community; a discussion on one tree can become invested as a fight over sustainability principles. As governance looks forward, as it has to deal with the issue of more or less desirable futures for the community, open concepts prove very useful in mediating the uncertainty of the future and adjusting it to the continuously produced present. If we would fully submit ourselves to the idea that the future is unknowable and that it is not possible to steer a community by means of policies and plans, then governance would be virtually impossible. Open concepts enable the capturing of desires of society in the face of an uncertain future. They allow projections of a good future, a means to get to our desires, even if this is impossible.

Open concepts, then, can be seen as productive fictions; fictions that are simply necessary in governance. Because of the multifaceted nature of governance, the versatility and various functions of open concepts can be easily observed. They can allow the governance process to continue even when there is no basic agreement, they allow actors to feign agreement or commitment, and allow them to make promises that cannot be kept. We can also speak, with Zizek, of disavowal (Zizek 2006): we might know better, but if all actors continue as if the newly introduced concept represents agreement it can actually produce that agreement.

6.3 Ideologies

With Zizek, we see ideologies not as veils over an objective reality, but rather as the discursive infrastructure of our political imagination (Zizek 1989). They are the narrative answers to the questions of good society, the values embedded, the modes of organisation and participation, the distribution of roles, and the forms of knowledge that bring such society closer. Ideologies in this view are narratives that might contain root metaphors and master signifiers. They are narratives that might produce many other narratives, metaphors and open concepts. Ideologies can delineate a discursive realm in which concepts and narratives, objects and subjects can travel without undergoing extreme transformations. They can amplify the effects of embedded narratives and concepts, and have, more than the embedded metaphors and open concepts, the power to open and close other narratives. They have the power of linking and disconnecting, because the similarities and dissimilarities suggested by them have much greater impact on a variety of discursive worlds and on society.

In governance, also in local governance, ideologies can transform everything. If new ideologies arrive, if new conflicts between existing ideologies arise, if the boundaries of ideologies harden for some reason, this can affect literally everything, up to the most minute detail in the most local governance arrangement. Objects can be transformed by ideological shifts or clashes, as can the functioning of metaphor, narrative and open concept. Everything can appear in a new light, in a re- politicization that makes restructuring of power/knowledge configurations necessary, and spurs new and more strategizing. What appeared as natural looks contingent and what appeared as consensus topics shows to be bones of contention.

In the next chapter we reflect on the reality effects of discourse, with emphasis on the role of discursive activity in governance on the construction of realities. Concepts, open concepts, metaphors, root metaphors, master signifiers, objects and subjects have effects on each other, on power relations, on what is experienced as reality. That our worlds are discursively constructed and that governance contributes to this, does by no means entail that every construct proposed in governance will be believed and that it will have reality effects in the community at large.

References

Abu-Lughod, L. (1992). *Writing women's worlds: Bedouin stories*. Berkeley: University of California Press.

Aristotle. (1954). *Aristotle: Rhetoric*. New York: Random House.

Aristotle & Lucas, D. W. (1972). *Poetics* (Repr. with corrections. ed.). Oxford: Clarendon Press.

Asimakou, T. (2009). *Innovation, knowledge and power in organizations*. Abingdon: Routledge.

Austin, J. L. (1962). *How to do things with words*. London: Clarendon Press.

Bal, M. (1985). *Narratology: Introduction to the theory of narrative*. Toronto: University of Toronto Press.

Bal, M. (2002). *Travelling concepts in the humanities: A rough guide*. Toronto: University of Toronto Press.

Barnes, T. J., & Duncan, J. S. (1992). *Writing worlds: Discourse, text and metaphor in the representation of landscape*. London: Routledge.

Beunen, R., & Hagens, J. E. (2009). The use of the concept of ecological networks in nature conservation policies and planning practices. *Landscape Research, 34*(5), 563–580.

Beunen, R., Van Assche, K., & Duineveld, M. (2013). Performing failure in conservation policy: The implementation of European Union directives in the Netherlands. *Land Use Policy, 31*, 280–288.

Czarniawska, B. (1998). *A narrative approach to organization studies*. Thousand Oaks: Sage.

Delanty, G. (2003). *Community*. London: Routledge.

Eco, U. (1976). *A theory of semiotics*. Bloomington: Indiana University Press.

Elias, N., & Scotson, J. L. (1994). *The established and the outsiders: A sociological enquiry into community problems*. London: Sage.

Elliot, A., & Du Gay, P. (Eds.). (2009). *Identity in a globalizing world*. London: Sage.

Foucault, M. (1973). *The order of things*. New York: Random House.

Gabriel, Y. (2000). *Storytelling in organizations. Facts, fictions, and fantasies*. Oxford: Oxford University Press.

Gunder, M., & Hillier, J. (2010). *Planning in ten words or less. A Lacanian entanglement with spatial planning*. Surrey: Ashgate.

Hajer, M. A. (1995). *The politics of environmental discourse: Ecological modernization and the policy process*. Oxford: Clarendon.

Jeffares, S. R. (2007). *Why public policy ideas catch on: Empty signifiers and flourishing neighbourhoods*. Birmingham: University of Birmingham.

Kooij, H., Van Assche, K., & Lagendijk, A. (2013). Open concepts as crystallization points and enablers of discursive configurations: The case of the innovation campus in the Nether-lands. *European Planning Studies, Online First*.

Lacan, J. (1977). *Écrits: A selection*. London: Tavistock Publications Limited.

Lakoff, G., & Johnson, M. (1980). *Metaphors we live by*. Chicago: University of Chicago Press.

Lévi-Strauss, C. (1968). *Structural anthropology*. London: Allen Lane.

MacKenzie, D., Muniesa, F., & Siu, L. (Eds.). (2007). *Do economists make markets? On the performativity of economics*. Princeton: Princeton University Press.

Rap, E. (2006). The success of a policy model: Irrigation management transfer in Mexico. *Journal of Development Studies, 42*(8), 1301–1324.

Sandercock, L. (2003). Out of the closet: The importance of stories and storytelling in planning practice. *Planning Theory and Practice, 4*, 11–28.

Seidl, D. (2005). *Organizational identity and self- transformation. An autopoietic perspective*. Aldershot: Ashgate.

Stavrakakis, Y. (1999). *Lacan and the political.* Abingdon: Routledge.
Van Assche, K., Beunen, R., & Duineveld, M. (2012). Performing failure and success: Dutch planning experiences. *Public Administration, 90*(3), 567–581.
Van Assche, K., Devlieger, P., Teampau, P., & Verschraegen, G. (2009). Forgetting and remembering in the margins: Constructing past and future in the Romanian Danube Delta. *Memory Studies, 2*(2), 211–234.
Van Assche, K., Duineveld, M., Beunen, R., & Teampau, P. (2011). Delineating locals: Transformations of knowledge/power and the governance of the Danube Delta. *Journal of Environmental Policy & Planning, 13*(1), 1–21.
Van Assche, K., Teampau, P., Devlieger, P., & Sucio, C. (2008). Liquid boundaries in marginal marshes. Reconstructions of identity in the Romanian Danube Delta. *Studia Sociologia, 39*(1), 115–138.
Zizek, S. (1989). *The sublime object of ideology*. London: Verso.
Zizek, S. (2006). *The parallax view*. Cambridge: MIT Press.

Chapter 7
Governance Paths and Reality Effects

Abstract In this chapter we investigate the reality effects of discourses in governance and discourses codified in policy. We distinguish between performance and performativity and acknowledge the importance of the discursive context. Next we discuss the performance and performativity exemplified by two special types of narratives, those claiming success and failure. The impact of narratives of success and failure on governance paths is examined.

7.1 Performance and Performativity

Performativity is an essential feature of the discursive construction and evolution of social worlds. Performativity implies that things appear true because of the evolvement of prior discourse (Butler 1997; Mackenzie et al. 2007). While the term *performativity* is often associated with the linguistic philosopher Austin and his theory of speech acts (Austin 1962), it led its own life in the post-structuralist traditions inspired by Foucault, Lacan and Deleuze (Beunen et al. 2013; Mackenzie et al. 2007; Van Assche et al. 2012b). We line up with this tradition: our realities are continuously black-boxed in the sense that we forget, hide or mask their constructed, contingent and temporal nature (Latour 1987). In this sense, everything we believe is the result of performativity, because everything is discursively constructed. This does not mean that every product of discourse is experienced as reality and becomes performative. People can recognize lies, and they can distinguish fiction from non-fiction.

Even fiction can become reality though. One can think of people modelling their behaviour on film stars, try to structure their life as a novel or a soap opera, or buy chocolates in the hope that the commercials promising a flourishing love life will turn out true (cf. Dill 2009). So, even when the distinction fiction/non-fiction is clear, the boundary is not impermeable. We can see why this is not strange: people create individual and group identities out of narrative, and narrative structures permeate both fiction and non- fiction genres. Because of structural

K. Van Assche et al., *Evolutionary Governance Theory*, SpringerBriefs in Economics,
DOI: 10.1007/978-3-319-00984-1_7,

similarity, and because of similarity in constructive mechanisms (everything being discourse), both structure and content of narrative can move easily between fiction and non-fiction, between self and group, and the stories can be consumed through various media. Societies construct borders between fiction and non-fiction, between self and story, to be able to function more easily in a simpler world that feels real. Yet these borders are contingent, and are continuously crossed because the same things happen on two sides, the same materials are being subjected to the same processes.

One can observe that narrative materials cross back and forth many times, between genres, between self, group and media. This crossing is not an innocent act. It potentially affects the reality experienced by many people. Therewith the power relations in a community can be affected in the sense that crossing necessarily transforms the narrative or some embedded elements, e.g. concepts and metaphors. The crossing can change the performativity: a life that is unexamined can reappear transformed in a soap series and afterwards become a positive or negative model for many. Some of the more persuasive aspects of soap series are certainly recognizable in real life, adapted from real lives, transformed, amplified and dramatized and condensed. They can then be projected back on the viewing community, where they can create reality effects of the sorts intimated. In other words, the differences in performativity of certain fictions can be explained by the different appeal of the borrowed non-fiction elements, and in other cases, the added appeal was created precisely in and by the fictionalization.

These boundary- crossings can be understood as a major source of performativity, but not the only one. Indeed, most interpretations of performativity emphasize the more simple mechanism of repetition, as mentioned above: things appear true because they have been presented as true for a while, and have not been questioned (Duineveld et al. 2013). Things can be repeated because of traditions, because of familiarity with founding epics and a common culture, or because experts present them (Fischer 1990). We refer back to the passages on object formation and stabilization for detail on a set of mechanisms at work in the creation of discursive objects and rendering them natural and evident.

Yet, even if these various mechanisms producing reality effects are certainly there, they usually do not work autonomously and they do not always have the same effect. Just as with a musical score or a film script, the power of narrative to alter our understanding of things crucially depends on the observed quality of the narrative and the observed quality of *performance*. Some stories are better than others, some feel more real than others, some have a stronger emotional or cognitive impact, or give the impression that they reveal something more profound about the human condition. This *revealing is at the same time constructing*. What it shows cannot be disentangled from what we believed before and what we believe after watching or reading. Moreover, it cannot be disentangled from how it is showed. Pre-existing reality and revealed reality are different, yet the revelation transforms the earlier version post- hoc. Form, content, and performance of the revelation work together here. The actor can show the essence of a deep experience for some, speaking certain words written by someone else, in a colour scheme devised by yet another person, but it is the whole scene that can have a revealing/transformative effect.

Performance can be characterized as people bringing narrative to life in unique embodied manners and it can be described as a process of interpretation and objectification of a narrative. This is necessarily a process of selection among alternatives and, possibly, the creation of a new interpretation. As in a post-structuralist understanding of the world everything is discursively constructed, everything is subjected to performance. The truth effects of everything in society hinge on its performance. In the literature on performance, a wide range of social practices have been deconstructed as performance: looking and remembering, identity or critique and theory (Hubbard 2008; Mackenzie et al. 2007). Closer to policy studies, steering, control, leadership and governance are demonstrated performance sites (Avid 2007; Szerszynski et al. 2003; Bialasiewicz et al. 2007; Hajer 2005, 2006; Rose 2002; Turnhout et al. 2010).

The effects of management actions, for example, can be greater if the manager plays the manager, moreover, the successful manager. People recognize certain narratives, mannerisms, types of behaviour as appertaining to 'the manager' and will orient themselves to this. Performance of leadership by managers can include formulation of bold and simple visions, overconfidence, risk-taking, a way of dressing, and many other things (Czarniawska-Joerges 2008; Gabriel 2000). The manager can be aware of some of these features, unaware of others. Societies have different versions of 'the manager' or 'the leader', so performances and performativity will differ accordingly. Some managers will perform the manager more convincingly, and certainly, after a while, certain results will have to be demonstrated. But proving success is part of the performance, and success is of course also measured in ways that are contingent, and sensitive to narrative transformation.

What makes it harder to assess the results of the manager, to distinguish them from the 'mere performance' is that various performances imply each other and can have performative effects that reinforce each other. The performance of leadership by managers, accompanied by fictions of control and overview and ascriptions of individual intention to whatever result the organization presents, is also a performance of steering (cf. Czarniawska-Joerges 2008). It is probably linked with performances of success and of innovation, systematically presenting things better and newer than they are. One can also expect a performance of expertise, of management expertise, a performance that has had strong reality effects since the managerial revolution of the 50 s, when the fiction spread that management skills are independent of context and content, a fiction that became the bread and butter of management schools, where managers are trained with the seal of approval of the university, and therefore, another claim to truth (cf. Burawoy 2001). Discursive configurations that already mutually support each other, that are mutually imbricated and have had performative effects before, can underpin the embedded aspects of performances that are synthesized in the figure of the leader or the manager. In modern society, the character of the manager has taken over much of the mythology of leadership, while conversely, the manager acquired some of the mythical traits of older leader figures.

In modern society, the truth effects of performance are likely to be catalysed by subsumption in a structure of roles (such as the manager). The pose of sincerity as a performance of authenticity can be made superfluous once truth is associated with routinized roles. The importance of performance in truth construction brings the *rhetorical context* to the foreground. It forces a reflection on the *positionality* of the performance: time, location, occasion, audience, genre and role must be interpreted correctly in order to persuade (Bourdieu 1991). Uniquely embodied performances can have unique performative effects, something that might have been forgotten in early, linguistically inspired versions of semiotics and post-structuralism. We are always part of an audience, absorbing some form of staged and ritualized behaviour, but that does not make it entirely reducible to the pattern of ritual.

Performance and performativity do not necessarily imply each other, but usually influence each other, and sometimes the mutual implication is there (Beunen et al. 2013). This entails that one cannot be regarded as a form of the other and that their empirical relation has to be established in each case. Performativity can be the result of strategic performance, of performance that became a second nature as result of socialization, it can be the consequence of naturalized concepts silently embedded in discourse, and of narratives and concepts crossing the boundaries of self, group and recognizable storytelling.

It also depends on the broader discursive configuration in which the issue at stake is embedded. In the USSR, planning mythologies were upheld by the Soviet ideologies, and there was less need to prove the reality effects of this or that plan (Taubman 1973; Van Assche et al. 2012a). In governance, where narratives and embedding narratives are continuously confronted and transformed, one can see performance of roles, one can see strategic manipulations of truth, and persuasive presentations of believed truths. One can also notice a wide variety of unintended performative effects of the narrative changes that are part and parcel of governance. A new narrative can be performative and therefore make embedded objects performative. A new narrative can be performative since it fits broader discursive configurations. A metaphor embedded in deeply rooted narrative can have new performative effects, open new vista's or create new objects, because of the existing embedding and-or the performance. Open concepts can be more productive when they generate meanings because of other resonating narratives.

7.2 Performing Failure and Success

In governance, some performances and some forms of performativity are more important than others. A special role is assigned for performances of failure and success, particularly in an environment where some accountability is expected and where success is deemed important (Van Assche et al. 2012b; Beunen et al. 2013; Vaara 2002; Rap 2006; Mosse 2005). Narratives of governance success and failure include recurring structural features: heroes and villains, dramatic episodes, driving forces and obstacles, a climax, spurring to further action (failure) or maintaining the balance (success). Stories about success and failure are part of a continually shifting discursive environment where the narrative can or cannot be linked to criteria, characters, story lines and events in other discourses. This discursive environment must be understood as the broader rhetorical context, the context of performance.

Policy narratives are almost certain to include institutionalized roles and discourses and they co-determine the potential success of a certain perspective on success and failure. New or decaying discourses in the environment and new discursive coalitions can contribute to the persuasiveness of a particular success or failure narrative. The more dominant a certain interpretation of success becomes, the harder it becomes to take alternative positions and the more likely it is to be institutionalized. Conversely, the more dominant a certain institution becomes, the more likely it is that the associated narratives will be performative.

Performances of success will thus be more successful when the narrative fits the discursive environment and when there is a narrative, rather than an isolated performance regarding an isolated object. In that case performativity is more likely. Performativity here, the generalized belief in success or failure, can stem from many sources, including the control over expertise, over measuring instruments and methods, over the debating arena, etc. Success stories can harden objects, institutions and expertise, and deconstruct others. The same is true for failure stories. Failure stories can prove things, just as success stories can, but the demonstration of failure renders the implicit alternative more true. Whereas success stories tend to make alternatives invisible, failure stories can either show or pave the way for better alternatives. The destructive potential of failure narratives can be fully unleashed against the observed failure. Yet this can amount to an argument contra a vested organizational and discursive order, an entrenched power/knowledge configuration, or it can become an argument to reinforce or reinvigorate that order: much work is left to do, let's get started now! In this sense, success and failure narratives are not entirely symmetrical. They can have similar conservative effects, but for transformative effects, one has to look primarily at failure stories.

From a social systems perspective a rhetoric of success and failure represents an attempt to spread the narrative of a network of observers to another network of observers (Fuchs 2001). Within governance these networks of observers are often organizations. Organizational communication can create ascriptions of other organizations and create "actors" it recognizes in its environment. Organizations can address each other, but what happens internally cannot be fully reconstructed using the reasoning of the observing system. For an external observer some of the different narratives might resemble each other, but the sharing of narratives cannot be assumed: "the similarity of distinctions across observers in a society is a contingent and improbable social outcome and accomplishment, not a transcendental a priori" (Fuchs 2001: 19). Organizations that co- evolve in a governance system, do acquire more insights in the neighbouring organizations, and crystallized roles for each organization reduce the need to fully comprehend the others.

A successful rhetoric of success or failure can be interpreted as a narrative that becomes shared by a number of organizations. In a governance system, the repeated interactions between members of these organizations make it easier for a narrative to spread. If other organizations can first of all make sense of the story of success or failure, and next embed it in their decision- making, then the narrative becomes shared, and the story of success or failure acquires a function in the organization. If many organizations start to operate under the same assumptions regarding success, both the success ascription and the underlying discursive configurations are becoming more real for more, and consequently they become harder to reflect upon and harder to change.

Success stories can thus harden the governance path, by keeping the underlying discursive configuration intact, by keeping actors and institutions in place, and by spurring new objects in line with the old order. The hardening of a path because of success performances also entails more systematic forgetting of alternatives, of alternative measuring methods, alternative perspectives, and alternative ideologies. Simplification of success measurement can sometimes lead to real transparency and comparison of perspectives and policy options, but it is more likely that the reduction of complexity became possible because of an already ideological selectivity that is slanted in one direction.

Quantification and commensuration deserves a special mention here as a reductionist tool (Espeland and Stevens 1998; Scott 1998). In these processes the actions of actors and their results are reduced to a set of numbers and targets, and these numbers are the basis of evaluation (cf. Scott 1995; Jacobs 1961). In many cases, actions that are not easy to quantify are not evaluated and they might be marginalized because of that. Actions and results that are qualitatively different can be reduced to numbers in the same set and treated as if they are comparable, as if they are commensurate. Actors might shift their focus to these indicators of success and therewith the underlying substantive goals might get out of sight. The functioning of the organization is then transformed by the tools used create a false transparency. If governments, and governance more broadly, copy this set of assumptions from the private sector (e.g. under the banner of new public management), then the decisions that are supposed to represent and serve the community are structured by numbers that probably miss many issues deemed important in the community, and that do not indicate many effects, positive and negative, of prior policies (Van Ark 2005).

The example of commensuration also indicates however that performances of success underpinned by certain measurement methods can come down because of that association. If organizations reinterpret themselves as successful by looking at a new set of indicators, and start to follow those indicators more closely, gear themselves completely towards these numbers, and publicize their performance on this dimension, then they make themselves dependent on the numbers and the method. The creation of success by means of close association with a methodology, is the anticipation of a new kind of failure. This is the case because one cannot fully control the method, and one time or another, the numbers will look bad. One can deduce that performances of success can harden the evolutionary path of an organization (or of a governance arrangement), but that the conceptual instruments that are utilized can produce failure -after which a new path might be taken.

In governance, one can also mention the damaging effects of performances of transparency, as a goal in itself, and of success and failure narratives regarding transparency. The focus on creating new fictions of transparency in a process that can never be transparent, derails attempts at finding common goods and solving community issues. A quantification of transparency, and a correlated measure of 'corruption', assumed to be the inverse concept, is not only methodologically questionable. It shifts the attention away from the substantive goals of a specific governance process, away from the potentially negative effects of real transparency on decision-making as negotiation, and from the potentially positive effects of various informal institutions lumped together under 'corruption'. Also in the case of policy success and failure, performance and performativity do not presuppose each other. Performances of success or failure can render a certain understanding of policy results real and they can render the narrative widely acceptable, but this does not happen automatically. The effects of performance cannot entirely be determined by a mere use of the formulaic narratives, routines, roles and rituals that seem to guarantee truth effects on a certain occasion.

In the next chapter, we take a step back and look at the results of so many different governance paths: widely diverging governance arrangements. Without downplaying the uniqueness of paths and the necessity to reconstruct and understand them, we present a way to categorize the results of these paths. This opens the door to Chap. 9, an overview of EGT where we re- articulate the relations between the key concepts.

References

Austin, J. L. (1962). *How to do things with words*. London: Clarendon Press.

Avid, A. P. (2007). Path dependence: a foundational concept for historical social science. *Cliometrica, 1*, 91–114.

Beunen, R., Van Assche, K., & Duineveld, M. (2013). Performing failure in conservation policy: The implementation of European Union directives in the Netherlands. *Land Use Policy, 31*, 280–288.

Bialasiewicz, L., Campbell, D., Elden, S., Graham, S., Jeffrey, A., & Williams, A. J. (2007). Performing security: The imaginative geographies of current US strategy. *Political Geography, 26*(4), 405–422.

Bourdieu, P. (1991). *Language and symbolic power*. Cambridge: Polity.

Burawoy, M. (2001). Transition without transformation: Russia's involutionary road to capitalism. *East European Politics and Societies, 15*(2), 269–290.

Butler, J. (1997). *Excitable speech: a politics of the performative*. New York: Routledge.

Czarniawska-Joerges, B. (2008). *A theory of organizing*. Cheltenham: Edward Elgar.

Dill, K. E. (2009). *How fantasy becomes reality: seeing through media influence*. Oxford: Oxford University Press.

Duineveld, M., Van Assche, K., & Beunen, R. (2013). Making things irreversible. Object stabilization in urban planning and design. *Geoforum, 46*, 16–24.

Espeland, W. N., & Stevens, M. L. (1998). Commensuration as a social process. *Annual Review of Sociology, 24*, 313–343.

Fischer, F. (1990). *Technocracy and the politics of expertise*. Newbury Park: Sage Publications.

Fuchs, S. (2001). *Against essentialism: a theory of culture and society*. Cambridge: Harvard University Press.

Gabriel, Y. (2000). *Storytelling in organizations. facts, fictions, and fantasies*. Oxford: Oxford University Press.

Hajer, M. (2005). Rebuilding ground zero. The politics of performance. *Planning Theory and Practice, 6*, 445–464.

Hajer, M. A. (2006). The living institutions of the EU: Analysing governance as performance. *Perspectives on European Politics and Society, 7*(1), 41–55.

Hubbard, P. (2008). Here, there, everywhere: The ubiquitous geographies of heteronormativity. *Geography Compass, 2*(3), 640–658.

Jacobs, J. (1961). *Death and life of great American cities*. Harmondsworth: Penguin.

Latour, B. (1987). *Science in action. How to follow scientists and engineers through society*. Cambridge: Harvard University Press.

MacKenzie, D., Muniesa, F., & Siu, L. (Eds.). (2007). *Do economists make markets?: On the performativity of economics*. Princeton: Princeton University Press.

Mosse, D. (2005). *Cultivating development: an ethnography of aid policy and practice*. London: Pluto Press.

Rap, E. (2006). The success of a policy model: Irrigation management transfer in Mexico. *Journal of Development Studies, 42*(8), 1301–1324.

Rose, M. (2002). The seductions of resistance: power, politics, and a performative style of systems. *Environment and Planning D: Society and Space, 20*, 383–400.

Scott, J. C. (1995). State Simplifications: Nature, space and people. *The Journal of Political Philosophy, 3*(3), 191–233.

Scott, J. C. (1998). *Seeing like a state: How certain schemes to improve the human condition have failed*. New Haven: Yale University Press.

Szerszynski, B., Heim, W., & Waterton, C. (2003). *Nature performed: environment, culture and performance*. Oxford: Blackwell Publishing.

Taubman, W. (1973). *Governing soviet cities. Bureaucratic politics and urban development in the USSR*. New York: Praeger.

Turnhout, E., Bommel, S., & van Aarts, N. (2010). How participation creates citizens: Participatory governance as performative practice. *Ecology and Society, 15*(4), 26.

Vaara, E. (2002). On the discursive construction of success/failure in narratives of post-merger integration. *Organization Studies, 23*(2), 211–248.

Van Ark, R. G. H. (2005). *Planning, contract en commitment: naar een relationeel perspectief op gebiedscontracten in de ruimtelijke planning*. Delft: Eburon.

Van Assche, K., Beunen, R., & Duineveld, M. (2012a). Performing failure and success: Dutch planning experiences. *Public Administration, 90*(3), 567–581.

Van Assche, K., Salukvadze, J., & Duineveld, M. (2012b). Speed, vitality and innovation in the reinvention of georgian planning aspects of integration and role formation. *European Planning Studies, 20*(6), 999–1015.

Part IV
Applying EGT

Chapter 8
Governance and Its Categories

Abstract In this chapter we elaborate on the situation after evolution and present a framework to analyse a world in which many governance paths have produced a wide variety of governance arrangements. Understanding the functioning of governance arrangements requires reconstruction of paths. Such reconstruction can be aided by a categorization of the resulting arrangements. We propose two ways to categorize, one for the larger scale, distinguishing governance models, and one for the smaller scale, distinguishing governance dimensions.

8.1 Governance Models

Over time numerous governance models have evolved in different territories and the models are in an on-going process of change. Different governance paths lead in different directions, although at the same time there are converging forces at work in world society: functional differentiation and the dissemination of narratives and embedded objects (Luhmann 2012; Stichweh 2000). From the previous chapters, it can be deduced that no model of governance is perfect, as in perfectly legitimate, efficient, and stable. The sources of instability are manifold and have been discussed already: power/knowledge configurations that transform in confrontation with others, actor/institution configurations that are similarly self-transformative, shifts in society that lead to the creation of new narratives or the reinterpretation of others, new actors that stand up, associated with old or new narratives, or actors that will introduce shifts in governance and will be transformed themselves. Actor/institution configurations are at the same time sources of stability. Indeed, it is this stabilizing function that made the evolution of society towards more complexity possible (Greif 2006). This stabilizing function is a precondition for functional differentiation (Luhmann 1990). Both actors and institutions are believed to be stable, and this productive fiction allows the proliferation of interactions and the formation of structures that makes specialization possible.

K. Van Assche et al., *Evolutionary Governance Theory*, SpringerBriefs in Economics,
DOI: 10.1007/978-3-319-00984-1_8, © The Author(s) 2014

As a result of both stabilizing and destabilizing functions, evolution is not chaos, and innovation and adaptation are possible (Luhmann 1989, 1990). It also means that the results of many evolutionary paths do show patterns that can be categorized. Many forms of markets, and models of democracies continue to function next to each other, yet it is possible to see a family likeness between some. If we look at a smaller scale, one can also distinguish different governance models that bear more or less resemblance to each other. Understanding governance requires understanding and reconstructing governance paths and the associated mechanisms described above. The categorization of the results of these different paths can assist the interpretation of reconstructions and it can also provide a shorthand for the understanding of certain features of governance arrangements.

From the political science literature, we adopt a categorization of models of democracy that distinguishes between *liberal democracy, social democracy/socialism, civic republicanism, civil society and communitarianism* (cf. Putman 1993; Young 2000; Fischer 2000; Goodin 2008; Guinier 1994; Held 1996; Holmes 1995). These models of democracy are types of outcomes of slow and large scale governance evolutions. Other categorizations are possible, but we consider this one useful for our present purposes, because it summarizes a vast body of political theory and it can be interpreted well in terms of long term governance paths and functional differentiation. These models are, as other theoretical constructs, borrowed from experienced realities, transformed in theory, and bounced back in reality. In this case this reality is a political practice that partly defines and transforms itself based on prevalent versions of concepts with a theoretical origin. The five models are seen as versions of democracy, i.e. represent developed polities marked by some level of functional differentiation. Empirically, most polities have features of several of these models, since history has several strands, and governance includes competing discourses, including on governance, but in many cases, one model dominates at a certain point in time, in a certain territory.

Liberal democracies are regimes based on a self-understanding of the community as a collection of individuals. Community is thus regarded a weak concept and individual autonomy tends to become more important than duties and obligations to each other or to the community at large. Individuals are the bearers first of all of rights, and the government is there to make sure that these rights are respected. Government is thus less about collective decision-making than about arbitrage in conflicts, and about setting the rules for this (North et al. 2009). If there is a conscious effort towards brokering of other sorts of collectively binding decisions, common goods are rarely invoked, and the issue is treated as a problem of aggregation of preferences. The state can easily become alienated from society in such perspective, and individuals have to be defended against the state. Governance is easily polarized as either too much or too less state interference, or polarized as either the complete local self-governance of libertarian fantasies or state oppression. Taxation easily appears as unfair and oppressive, since the common goods these taxes could be used for, are often not considered as such. Citizen participation is weak in this model in the sense that representation after voting is the prime mechanism of governance, yet this can be combined with extreme involvement in local communities that prefer to be left alone by the rest of the community and by higher level politics.

In much of the Anglo-Saxon literature, the Liberal democracy model is presented as 'the democracy', the only form of true democracy and the only correct and efficient coupling with 'the' market. Indeed, the free citizens of politics are ideally citizens engaged in market transactions, and their freedom is a freedom to do so in any way they want. Both individuals and markets are preferably lightly regulated, as they both develop best, in accordance with their respective natures, if left alone. Development of the community is economic development. Economic development takes place in a context where transactions are made easy by light regulation, and where that same lightness creates space for experiment and product innovation. It also creates innovation in transaction forms, financing schemes and organizational forms. 'The market' in this model is supposedly independent from the rest of society and of its own history. It is simply a space cleared from interference, an ideally empty space, and thus everywhere the same.

Social democracies/socialist regimes have a different understanding of history and community. In socialist regimes, a Marxian interpretation of history sees progress leading to revolution, after which the oppressed workers can liberate themselves and install a socialist regime. After this history stops, and, as with liberal democracy, a stable state ensues. Ideology, in the Marxist sense, is what blinded the oppressed classes before revolution, the narratives that made people forget the essence of reality, i.e. economic relations and their inferior position in them. Oppressed people need help though, some enlightened workers/intellectuals can guide them, tell them the truths they could not think themselves, and help them in organizing a society in which all are emancipated. Equality as members of the collective is a core value, and radical democracy is thought to be compatible with the collective moulding of the individual. The collective can show the individual what is good for herself, and what her best contribution to the collective could be. The collective in the most famous communist experiment, the USSR, was de facto replaced by the state, and the power behind the state was the Party, an elite with its own internal elite.

The state then comes to represent the people, and can define common goals that have to be implemented. Governance is mostly governance coordinating different governmental actors. Law, politics and economy are not highly differentiated, since government sees the way forward, the path towards communism, and has to mobilize the economic resources needed. Laws serve to regulate progress, the evolution of society towards communism, but as government knows the path, there is no need for an independent judicial apparatus. Autonomy of the legal system and autonomous markets are perceived as threatening development, possibly throwing back evolution to a state of bourgeois individualism.

Social democracies combine features of socialist regimes with some of the other models, often liberal democracy. Citizens are granted rights and do not participate much in governance, but government does revolve substantially about the articulation of policies and plans that can bring certain common goods closer. The visions are not those of a communist society as utopian end time, and they will change over time, but government is involved in the production of such visions, in which a variety of collective goods can be embedded. In most cases, government is also involved in the implementation of such visions, which necessitates large bureaucracies and/or large budget for those administrations to hire 'free' market players that can provide expertise and other services in the implementation process. And budgets mean taxes. As long as the community sees the common goods in ways similar to the government, and experiences the chosen policies as appropriate ways to work in that direction, taxation and government intervention can be found acceptable, a result of shared narratives.

Civil society regimes see society as a collection of organizations, rather than a collective or a collection of individuals. As liberal democracy, this is a 'small government' model, in which representation of individuals takes place through a different medium, in this case the organization. The internal selectivity of organizational decision-making, and the membership of people in several organizations is expected to have the overall result of fair representation of all people and ideas in the community. Government is a tiny desk where organizations meet, where they plea for influence on rule-making, making a case that modifications to laws, policies and plans would benefit not only themselves but also the community. Different variations of civil society emphasize for profit organizations (businesses) or non-profit organizations as the key players. Most proponents in the academic literature highlight the positive effects of self-organization combined with higher-level lobbying of these voluntary associations. Yet they do not seem to perceive that the proposed model is structurally the same as the deplored one, where big business meets government behind closed doors. Once this form of coordination of governance is entrenched, and non-profits know the way, there is no reason to assume that business will not find the way.

While the argument was made earlier that absolute transparency in governance is impossible and that striving for absolute transparency as a goal in itself can have various unpleasant side effects, we want to make the case that civil society regimes are extremely opaque. The tiny desk of government has only a few people at a time gathered around it, and sits in a tiny room with closed doors. Lobby discussions replace parliamentary debate or other forms of public debate in other governance sites. It is impossible to know who exactly talked to officials, who was left out, and which criteria of deliberation were used to determine influence on rule-making. Participation is primarily participation in organizations, but this participation is uneven. If this participatory mechanism replaces or undermines other forms of representation, the distribution of power and the benefits of power in society is likely to alter without the community being aware of it. Thus, the model structurally reduces transparency, and this has a set of negative side effects that can be just as harmful than the ones stemming from fetishizing transparency. One negative effect can be that slowly evolved functional differentiation is undermined. The autonomy of politics versus law and economy can be jeopardized when certain interests are granted different legal and political treatment.

Communitarian regimes understand society as a collection of small communities. In some versions, society beyond the level of the village or small town disappears beyond the horizon, and the village becomes the world. Individuals are first of all member of these communities, and at that level, government can play a substantial role. Higher level government is minimal, a minimal form of coordination of potentially very different and competing communities. Social life takes places at a small scale, in a small community dense with social networks, a community that imposes its order and traditions but also offers networks of mutual support. Duties accompany freedoms. Individual choices are shaped and constrained by the discursive worlds of the communities, their actor/network configurations, often rich in informal institutions, and their power/knowledge configurations, often involving local elites and leader figures (priest, chief, mayor, elders, leading families).

Communitarian regimes can easily switch between utopia and dystopia. The duality of small town life has been discerned in American popular culture, where for each movie glorifying nostalgically the apple pie baked by the neighbours, there is a movie showing mercilessly the continuous interference by neighbours imposing their values. In American culture, this ambiguity is reinforced by a widespread appreciation of self-reinvention as essential to American life. The communitarian ideal of small town life sits uneasily in America with the imposition of rules and roles on its residents, the pressure to fit an accepted role and the obstacles to choose a different identity. Growing up is often moving. In general, one can speak of a potential for internal oppression and external hostility. The world can be small, stringently structured inside, and the unknown outside easily looks strange, different, and offensive to the values held dearly. The closed character of communities does not enhance reflexivity and innovation; what looks very true in a small place can easily dissipate into opinion in a bigger world, and this can be a reason to eschew that bigger world, or to be very upset with the neighbouring part of that world.

In terms of differentiation, one can say that a communitarian society represents a risk of undermining functional differentiation. It might throw back society to a less developed state, a collection of villages without much communication, without incorporation in a world that enables scientific, legal, political, artistic specialized discourse, a world with separation of powers and separation of church, state and markets. Politics can easily slip into segmentary and hierarchical modes, local markets can be controlled by politics or vice versa; local religious figures can exert political influence and undermine due legal process. It is not so much the local character that carries these risks, as the closed character. Functional differentiation is the result and cause of an opening of communities, as discursive worlds with political, economic and legal structures. It required and caused a break with the grip of tradition over community life and individual development. Nostalgia for an imagined time of personalized relations and communities as warm nests can make people forget the reasons for the development of impersonal rules and roles.

Civic republican regimes assume that a strong individual and a strong state can go together. People are expected to be deeply engaged in governance, as individuals, as members of organizations, of parties, as voters, as participants in public debate. Citizens need to be informed, and the quality of education and media is essential for the quality of democracy. Participation is expected, is a civic duty, and takes places through these various channels. Different forms of participation can find a place in different sites of governance, and can be linked to different aspects of identity. The complexity of identity is hence not perceived as a problem, but as an asset, since it makes it natural to be active in different roles, and this diversity of engagement lowers the chance that politics is reduced to identity politics. It represents a valuable form of checks and balances, because it makes it unlikely that one actor in governance can amass too much power and dominate decision-making. Since individuals are internally divided, they tend to side with different actors depending on the occasion, and they will tend to maintain a variety of actors and sorts of actors in politics.

For civic republicanism, private initiative ought to be encouraged, yet individual wealth is tricky for the community, since it can easily corrupt governance, e.g. by creating Potemkin actors or by simply buying existing actors. Machiavelli, a main inspiration for civic republicanism, famously stated that the state should be rich and citizens kept poor (Machiavelli 1988). Besides managing the risk of corruption, the taxation involved can serve positive purposes, i.e. the furthering of common goods. These common goods are continuously redefined in the daily friction of participatory governance, and so are the visions to substantiate them. On-going conflict and self-transformation are not seen as a governance problem. On the contrary, it is the essence of democracy in this perspective. It is the practical realization of the principle of strong citizens in a strong state.

Laws, in this perspective, do not maintain themselves, and policies and plans do not implement themselves. Permanent scrutiny of government action is needed, as well as continuous observation and enforcement by government. An intricate web of checks and balances can lower the risk of corruption of government and non-enforcement of rules. Laws cannot be perfect or perfectly stable either, as there is no perfect and perfectly stable order in society, nor a natural order of things that would prescribe social organization by means of natural law. Good laws are adaptable laws, adaptable to changes in the internal and external circumstances, to changing contexts of military and economic necessity, changing values, desires, powers and possibilities inside and outside.

These five models have both theoretical and empirical origins, and they had both theoretical and practical effects. Insofar as they are discursive constructs, they are ideal models that do not exist in pure form in empirical reality. Insofar as they are inspired by observed practices and had influence on governance practice for centuries, they are observable in the worlds of governance. As we understand societies as autopoietic social systems consisting of other such systems, all structures and elements are reshaped over time, and even these basic categories can change over time. Societies can move from civic republicanism to liberal democracy, such as the US, and they can see local revivals that resemble communitarianism, as in that same US. As autopoietic reproduction is marked by path dependencies, interdependencies and goal dependencies, and since communities are never entirely dominated by one discourse, it is almost certain that at any given point in time, one can discern features of different models in a society. These features can be ascribed both to old internal variation and to traces of paradigmatic models from the past. Discerning whether civic republican features can be explained best by reference to an evolutionary strand that was there from the beginning, as a second or third voice, or whether it is a leftover from a mode of organization that was once dominant, requires mapping of the evolutionary paths of governance.

The models represent and simplify different paths of evolution as different modes of structural coupling between politics, law and economy. They can also be seen as different compositions of basic concepts that seem shared by most models, in theory and in practice. Individuals, organizations, communities, government, citizens, rights and duties, participation and representation, law, markets, politics, private and public goods are recurring concepts. These concepts can be found in the theoretical models, but also in the historical self-descriptions of most western societies since the renaissance. The models can be understood then as understandings of commonly observed differences in the linkages between individual and community, small community and larger community (in the nascent nation states), personal ties and impersonal roles. They each represent a different narrative on what is there and what ought to be there, on existing and ideal societies and their modes of organization. Some narratives proved more persuasive than others to incite change. Change in governance could be trigged by these narratives because they fit existing practices while showing small differences, or because they showed differences from existing practices that were persuasive because of resonances with other discursive and practical evolutions. A new class with a new perspective might have emerged, and a model that looks very different from what they see around them might be very persuasive because of that difference and because of the similarity with some of their core convictions.

Each model is in theory compatible with functional differentiation, albeit under a different set of couplings. They all recognize markets, even socialism, but their internal structure, as well as the relation with politics and law will be interpreted differently. Liberal democracy believes in 'the' market, as the space left open by government. Communitarianism sees the market as that domain of economic interactions that requires money and impersonal roles (buyer, seller, banker), a domain ideally smaller than that of informal exchange. It is ideally also a local domain: buy local. For socialism, the market is a small domain that takes care of the goods that government cannot provide because the transaction costs would be too high: it is impossible to decide who needs how many carrots and to grow and distribute those carrots accordingly. In a civil society model, the market is only free in the sense that free access to government might be asked for businesses and industry groups. The market is structured as competition between organizations and associations of organizations, in fact as much a competition for market share as a competition for privileged access to rule-making. For civic republicanism, the market is both shaping and shaped by politics, and as such in constant transformation. Individual initiative should be rewarded, making money made possible and encouraged, but a fair share of profits should be skimmed off to support and improve the community, and to keep everybody honest.

These five models are thus to be seen as shorthands for an interpretation of the results of governance paths over a long period of time. They represent some reoccurring patterns of coupling between function systems, associated with often reoccurring patterns of coupling between basic concepts of political self-description. Each permutation of the basic concepts fits a narrative of good society. Applying the models does not lessen the need for a reconstruction of governance paths. They can be part of such reconstruction and they can give a quick impression of some key characteristics of a given governance arrangement in a larger area.

We propose a different, compatible approach for the analysis of faster and smaller evolutions, based on the concept of governance dimensions. However, we do not want to over-emphasize the scale distinction. An analysis based on dimensions can also give more detail to analyses based on functional couplings and foundational narratives. The major difference is that the crystallization of structural couplings and the associated categories of narratives on self and community takes time, and cannot always be easily observed on the small scale, without a study of the larger scale as context.

8.2 Governance Dimensions

We can describe each governance arrangement by means of a set of choice dimensions. We distinguish four dimensions that are relevant for governance: types of institutions, forms of democracy, forms of steering and knowledge mobilized. This, too, is a post-hoc approach that draws upon analysing and categorizing governance paths. This means that it cannot be used without reconstruction of the governance paths. It is, however, a more refined instrument than the first analysis offered by means of the five models of democracy and their narrative structure.

Governance evolution is radical in the sense that the configuration of actors/institutions and power/knowledge, and in fact the whole machinery of narratively constructed worlds, are all the product of evolution. It is a complex process involving a variety of decision-making premises for each actor and for the collective of actors. Decision-making relates to different dimensions of governance. Since at least at certain points during governance evolution the positions on the dimensions taken in a certain community are the result of choice, we speak of choice dimensions. Both the dimensions that are considered important as well as the alternative positions on these dimensions show recurring patterns. Certain dimensions and clusters of dimensions will be more common than others. Much work can for example be found on the relation between the forms of democracy and knowledge mobilisation (Dryzek 2000; Fischer 2009; Foucault 2003; Latour 2004) or on the relation between institutions and steering (Easterly 2006; North et al. 2009; Pierre 2000). One can see that the major alternative positions that appear on these dimensions show patterns of repetition. As with the models of democracy, this can have a variety of reasons, including, but not limited to, underlying patterns of structural coupling, shared or competing narratives (leading to polarized positions on dimensions), and shared conceptual basics to think of self and community.

Within governance four choice dimensions often appear as important for decision-making and they often occur together: *types of institutions*, *forms of democracy*, *forms of steering and knowledge mobilized.* The positions taken on them can certainly differ, but a cluster of oppositions can be seen to reoccur often: *formal vs. informal institutions*; *representative vs. participatory democracy*; *central steering vs. network steering and expert knowledge vs. local knowledge.* More and different positions are possible on each dimension, but at least in the west the *image in communities of the choice* is often polarized in these opposite terms. The practices of decision-making might differ from the ways they are imaged or presented. Decision-making, for example might be driven by a different set of institutions, e.g. more by informality than acknowledged, more by local knowledge than assumed, or in fact not so much by knowledge as by traditional precept (Fischer 2000; Scott 1998; Jacobs 1961). Sometimes, the self-image of coordination is closer to the actual coordination than in other communities. Sometimes, the choices are understood as more stark and polarized than elsewhere. Sometimes, the choice was more clearly a choice, in other places a position was silently taken, or it quietly emerged.

The term choice dimension is thus partly metaphorical. It does not always imply a conscious choice in a community, but rather a set of *bifurcations in the governance path* that turn out to be important for its later evolution, with the further complication that the actual pattern of evolution might differ from what is believed to be the case internally. The choice dimensions marking certain outcomes of governance evolutions are indeed outcomes of evolution: they do not appear immediately, they develop over time as actors react to each other and to the environment they confront. They can therefore be seen as an example of emergent structure in evolution. The configuration of relevant dimensions in the self-reproduction of a governance arrangement is an outcome of a history of interactions between actors, a history of transformation of actors and the rules of coordination they adopt. The same applies for the positions taken on these dimensions. What renders a certain configuration at once more cohesive and more of a signature for a given governance path, is that the dimensions and the chosen positions co-evolve. This is a strong form of co-evolution, not merely the result of the passive presence of others that somehow had to be calculated in, but the direct influence of events in other dimensions on the options in one dimension. The prevailing position on one dimension makes some positions on other dimensions impossible or less attractive. The importance of one dimension in collective decision-making renders it more or less likely that other dimensions will become or remain relevant. This process leads to a dependency in governance -a combination of path dependence and interdependence- that has often been overlooked in the academic literature.

Usually, positions on one dimension (e.g. degrees of participation) are analysed separately to assess governance arrangements. Choices on one dimension, however have effects for choices or positions on the others. This takes place in an evolution where choices for basic concepts and their relations tend to harden themselves once adopted in actor/institution evolutions and power/knowledge configurations. Once a set of choices in a set of dimensions is in place, this represents an additional and powerful conservative interdependence: the choices keep each other in place and they keep the dimension set in place. Once things are organized and understood in a certain manner, embedded in basic choices that have many different effects on social life, it is hard to change them. Cohesive sets of choices make it harder to change one choice. This form of interdependence represent a major path dependence in governance evolution. We can maybe understand the linkage between the dimensions more easily if we picture them as connected by a dynamic discursive world marked by two essential configurations we already met: power/knowledge and actor/institution.

We already know that in each configuration the two sides shape each other in a dialectical process. Formal coordination mechanisms shape the spaces and forms of informality and vice versa; configurations of actors shape and are shaped by the institutions they use to coordinate their interactions. Now we can say that choices on one governance dimension, the positions taken there, are likely to induce changes in the two configurations and in the linkage between them. This is likely to spark off changes above the surface again, in the more directly observable governance dimensions. Power/knowledge and actor/institution have to be understood then as dialectically engaged themselves, as two interlinked processes each incorporating other processes. One can speak of a meta-configuration. This meta-configuration can also be labelled as the identity of the evolution of a governance regime, the identity of a path, in other words. That identity itself is never entirely to be grasped, but one of the ways in which we can reconstruct it -besides path mapping- is studying the more easily visible interactions between choice dimensions. How dimensions are linked and how they respond to change on other dimensions, is revealing for the functioning of higher- level configurations in the autopoiesis of governance.

Let us give some examples of how the dialectics between governance dimensions can play out. A certain event, a disaster, for example can prompt more forms of central steering. These changing forms of steering can subsequently reshape the roles of knowledge, which impact power distributions, which affects the roles of (in)formality, which in turn has effects on the roles of actors and thus on the participation/representation balance, et cetera, ad infinitum. In the same way a new narrative on good society can alter the forms of knowledge inserted in governance and bring new actors to the table. Those actors expose existing forms of informal coordination as 'corruption' and bring the press to each meeting under the motto of 'transparency'. Since they are better in dealing with the press, they can erase the existing spaces for informal coordination, and impose their own form of informality on the others: instead of the big backroom, their own backroom. This marginalizes certain actors, and increases the influence of the new actors on rule-making, which makes it possible to formalize some of the new informalities, while keeping others under the table. E.g., instead of economists, ecologists are now the favourite advisors. Since the new actors believe to represent an absolute truth, the truth of green sustainable society, there is no need to continue existing forms of participation, and it seems more safe and efficient to revert to representation as the dominant form of citizen involvement and to central steering whenever possible.

Another example can be given about the implementation of a European Union nature conservation directive, where performances of failure spread over the actors and gained real impact (Beunen et al. 2013). After a conservation organisation won a court case against the development of a business park, the European Union directive became an important legal tool in decision-making practices. As a consequence decision-making shifted towards formality and legal expertise became more important. This expertise shaped the direction of solutions that were put forward, placing emphasis on legal clarity, but in strong relation with the position that decision- making could be steered by the government. This led to planning processes on site level in which other actors were invited as participants. These other actors, however hardly influenced decision making and their knowledge was largely ignored because of the top-down character and the strong focus on formal institutions and scientific knowledge.

An exogenous or endogenous change in circumstances can prompt changes in position on one dimension, which will have repercussions for the positions on other dimensions, because they intervene in the dynamics of underlying power/knowledge and actor/institution configurations. Positions on a dimension (the choice for one option at one bifurcation) affect underlying *processes*, the dialectics in configurations, which have effects elsewhere above the surface, back in the realm of visible paths, where the altered configurations exert pressure regarding the position on another dimension. The underlying configurations pressure the reconsideration of one choice, the choice for another option at another bifurcation. The two configurations thus connect the four dimensions in the manner of an infrastructure that is itself constantly in turmoil.

The metaphor of the furcating paths and routes that can be altered by pressure from below, shows that there are conservative counter- pressures on each occasion. The paths themselves appear now as multi- dimensional, following routes through n- dimensional spaces. Routes can be altered, but the set of dimensions and choices in place does function as such conservative counter- force, as a stabilizing mechanism for governance arrangements -which makes it useful for the analyst later to study governance types. More fundamentally, routes can be altered, but the new choices on one dimension can never be the same, can never have the same effects as similar choices earlier on the path. Routes and choices can never be entirely undone, as the past cannot be repeated in paths that are governed by path dependence, interdependence and goal dependence, paths where furthermore every element and structure is transformed along the way.

8.3 Spatial Scales: Individuals, Organizations, Communities

In the previous sections we have treated new modes of categorization as a first type of application of EGT. After discussing models of structural coupling and narrative permutation and categorization by means of sets of choice dimensions, we briefly discuss a third way of categorizing governance. This is a very traditional way that nevertheless looks different in our evolutionary perspective: spatial scales. For EGT, governance is always multi- level governance. This implies that a governance path is always embedded in other paths and that slow evolutions incorporate faster evolutions. In systems terms we can see the slow evolutions towards functional differentiation in a world society. This world society is marked by regional variations regarding the traces left of segmentary and hierarchical modes of differentiation. This regional variation is visible in different patterns of structural coupling. These patterns affect and are affected by smaller scale governance evolutions, that can reinforce or undermine certain couplings between law, economy and politics, and can strengthen or undermine the remaining forms of segmentary and hierarchical differentiation. Also organizational and functional differentiation reinforce each other and therewith form another link between scales of governance.

The spatial and time scales of governance are not given in nature. They too are discursive products. Discursive dynamics creates scales but also crosses scales. The rhythms of governance and the nesting of territories covered are the result of governance itself. What has been said earlier about the parallel articulation of action and discourse, about the invisible roles of the material world in boundary formation and about the mechanics of boundary crossing as world- creation, all applies to the topic of segmentation of time and space in and by governance. Material units can inspire governance units, but this can never be traced. A logic of practice, e.g. based on claimed administrative efficiency, is always tinged by discursive evolutions, by power/knowledge configurations structuring the concepts that become markers of the master signifier of efficiency. Internal experience with difficulties of coordination mingle with external narratives of good governance, the good life and the ideal community. These mechanisms also apply to the production of time scales: the arguments and strategies for bigger or smaller also apply to faster or slower. As Swyngedouw and others have demonstrated, power/knowledge configurations can both consciously and unwittingly produce scale effects (Swyngedouw et al. 2002). Large corporations with national ties can deliberately undermine local governance, but the globalization deplored by so many academic observers is to a large extent a byproduct of power/knowledge configurations that accompany an open world structured along lines of functional differentiation.

Governance creates its own spatial and temporal boundaries. Yet new narratives that can send governance on a different path can originate anywhere, independent of these scales. We can point the finger at the already mentioned secret homogeneity and fluidity of social life, bestowed upon it by the discursive nature of everything. Discourse can travel, can cross boundaries because in essence the other side is the same. Boundaries have effects because of a suspension of disbelief, because a community decides to believe that the two sides are different. This is a description of the mode of performativity typical for boundaries.

What happens when discourse still travels, across boundaries, is that communities and individuals are surprised. Since they do not assume that things can travel across boundaries, e.g. boundaries associated with scale, they do not observe such discursive migration. They experience the effects of a certain domain of discourse being structured differently. Usually, people are not aware that things changed, and if they are, the why is a riddle. Things just look and feel different than before, more or less natural, or desirable. A posteriori, rational explanations are furthered: sure, we need to change this policy, since it clearly did not work.

Reconstruction of governance paths and mapping the broader contexts can help to elucidate how discourse travelled across scales and influenced governance. Narratives, concepts, metaphors, objects, or ideas on coordinative rules based on these narratives et cetera can travel back and forth across scales, and between places. They can originate with a group, within an organization or with an individual. They can trickle down or move up. It can even be the case that a search for self within one individual creates a new image of a place, an area, of a community or communities in general. After interactions with others, via writing, or in other ways, alters broader discourses, creates new objects, and leads to the formation of new policies or to new actor/institution configurations and governance paths. One can think of environmental writers who first of all struggled with themselves, found meaning and identity in a life in nature and in writing about it, but at the same time created a new concept of nature and life that was disseminated by these writings. The life was maybe emulated by some, admired by more, and the care for nature (newly minted) possibly inspired new environmental policies, and a special care for the natural area made famous by the seminal writing. One can also think of 17th century landscape painters and poets, who inspired early 18th century landscape architects working for rich clients, doing things that proved inspirational for 19th century city councils in greening their cities and treating the city even as a continuation of the landscape.

Analysing governance in an EGT perspective in terms of scalar categories is therefore possible and interesting. However, what is even more telling about governance paths are the mechanisms of boundary crossing and the histories of discursive migration across scales. What travels can in some cases inspire new rules of coordination, but in most cases one can expect new narratives that inspire new desires and fears, carrying with them suggestions to deal with the realities reinterpreted by those desires and fears. Calls to action can come sooner or later, they can target governance arena's directly, or have indirect effects through a slow transformation of certain actors. Or, they can lead to the scattered emergence of new forms of local informal governance, which can in turn lead to new formal arrangements, or to a situation in which local informalities and thus differences are more tolerated in higher level- governance. New forms of expertise can start to dominate in the governance of a certain topic or a certain area, the linkages between social, spatial and conceptual boundaries can alter in the process (which in turn…).

References

Beunen, R., Van Assche, K., & Duineveld, M. (2013). Performing failure in conservation policy: The implementation of European Union directives in the Netherlands. *Land Use Policy, 31*, 280–288.

Dryzek, J. (2000). *Deliberative democracy and beyond*. Oxford: Oxford University Press.

Easterly, W. (2006). *The white man's burden: why the West's efforts to aid the rest have done so much ill and so little good*. Oxford: Oxford University Press.

Fischer, F. (2000). *Citizens, experts and the environment. The politics of local knowledge*. Durham: Duke University Press.

Fischer, F. (2009). *Democracy and expertise: Reorienting policy inquiry*. Oxford: Oxford University Press.
Foucault, M. (2003). *Society must be defended: Lectures at the College de France, 1975–76*. London: Allen Lane The Penguin Press.
Goodin, R. (2008). *Innovating democracy: democratic theory and practice after the deliberative turn* Oxford: Oxford University Press.
Greif, A. (2006). *Institutions and the path to the modern economy: Lessons from medieval trade*. Cambridge: Cambridge University Press.
Guinier, L. (1994). *The tyranny of the majority: fundamental fairness in representative democracy*. New York: Free Press.
Held, D. (1996). *Models of democracy* (2nd ed.). Cambridge: Polity.
Holmes, S. (1995). *Passions and constraint: On the theory of liberal democracy*. Chicago: University of Chicago Press.
Jacobs, J. (1961). *Death and life of great American cities*. Harmondsworth: Penguin.
Latour, B. (2004). *Politics of nature. How to bring the sciences into democracy*. Cambridge: Harvard University Press.
Luhmann, N. (1989). *Ecological communication*. Chicago: University of Chicago Press.
Luhmann, N. (1990). *Political theory in the welfare state*. Berlin: Mouton de Gruyter.
Luhmann, N. (2012). *Theory of society (Vol. 1). Cultural memory in the present*. Stanford: Stanford University Press.
Machiavelli, N. (1988). *The prince*. Cambridge: Cambridge University Press.
North, D., Wallis, J., & Weingast, B. (2009). *Violence and social orders. a conceptual framework for interpreting recorded human history*. Cambridge: Cambrigde University Press.
Pierre, J. (2000). *Debating governance, authority, steering, and democracy*. Oxford: Oxford University Press.
Putman, R. (1993). *Making democracy work. Civic traditions in modern Italy*. Princeton: Princeton University Press.
Scott, J. C. (1998). *Seeing like a state: How certain schemes to improve the human condition have failed*. New Haven: Yale University Press.
Stichweh, R. (2000). *Die weltgesellschaft. Soziologische analysen*. Frankfurt: Suhrkamp.
Swyngedouw, E., Moulaer, F., & Rodriguez, A. (2002). Large scale urban development projects and local governance: From democratic urban planning to besieged local governance. *Geographische Zeitschrift, 89*(2+3), 69–84.
Young, I. M. (2000). *Inclusion and democracy*. Oxford: Oxford University Press.

Chapter 9
Overview of the EGT Model

Abstract In this chapter we bring together a series of the concepts presented earlier in a brief synthesis of EGT. Actor/institution and power/knowledge configurations are presented as the fundamental concepts shaping the development of governance paths.

EGT is an unfinished project, a project with great potential. At this point in its development, we can present however a very rich conceptual frame that encapsulates the key features and essential building blocks of EGT. The frame is new, and many of its building blocks are new, while others are derived from existing strands of theory, either taken directly or reinterpreted to fit EGT. We briefly present the key concepts again in their relation. For full elaboration of the concepts, their relations, and the linkages with secondary and tertiary concepts, please consult the respective chapters and some of the literature referred to. For the application of EGT on different topics and in different domains of policy, different combinations of these concepts will require highlighting and new methodological variations will have to be developed.

Governance is the coordination of collectively binding decisions for a community. Everything in governance is the result of evolution: actors, institutions, organizations, and discourses. Governance also affects the evolution of these elements. It introduces a cohesion that can be understood as co-evolution. Not all elements are the product of governance, but once they enter governance they will be transformed in and through governance.

9.1 Configurations of Actors, Institutions and Power/Knowledge

Decision-making requires coordination of actors by means of rules, by means of institutions. Governance deals with institutions and produces institutions: policies, plans and laws for example. Governance then coordinates actors who need

K. Van Assche et al., *Evolutionary Governance Theory*, SpringerBriefs in Economics,
DOI: 10.1007/978-3-319-00984-1_9, © The Author(s) 2014

to come to an accord, but the institutions also coordinate practices outside the governance arena, and they coordinate other institutions. We distinguish between formal, informal and dead institutions (Van Assche et al. 2012). Dead institutions have a strongest presence in old bureaucracies with a strong memory; they are institutions that lost their coordinative power, but that can be revived. Formal institutions are the ones that are supposed to coordinate action on a given occasion while informal ones are alternatives. Formal and informal institutions are in a dialectical relation (North 1990, 2005). Dialectics is a process whereby formal and informal transform each other; the functioning, form and space for formality is defined by informality and vice versa. Because of that, when assessing governance arrangements, it is preferable to look at the *configurations* of formal and informal institutions, the specific imbrication of formal, informal and dead that resulted from a specific governance evolution. Rather than assessing formal or informal, it is better to assess the results of the configuration in materializing certain common goods or solving community problems. These results can become visible only later, only partially, and in unexpected places.

A second configuration, encompassing the formal/informal configuration, is the *actor/institution configuration*. One can think of nested processes. Formal and informal shape each other in a configuration that stands in a similarly dialectical relation to actors. Actors will transform in governance, as a result of the manner in which they are coordinated and the manner in which they coordinate (cf. Hacking 1999). The continuous confrontation with others, their strategies and ideas, in the production of policies, plans and laws, will inevitably change an actor. Redefined actors will handle institutions differently and participate differently in the production of new institutions, introducing shifts in the institutional configuration, which then likely pressures actors into a new phase of reinvention.

A third configuration is the *power/knowledge configuration*. The way things are understood cannot be separated from the way situations are controlled. Conversely, the exercise of power requires and produces knowledge (Foucault 1998, 1979, 1994). Governance is always competition between actors, and confrontation with their strategies and understanding of the world. Confrontation, competition, but also cooperation and compromise can be analysed as continuous transformations of power/knowledge. New insights can lead to a new position in the governance game, while the game can lead to new insights (Van Assche et al. 2013). One can learn from other actors, and on other occasions learn new things or cling to old ideas to demarcate oneself as different, or even to polarize or escalate the situation (for strategic reasons). The pattern of learning is partly determined by the rules: a certain institutional configuration can make it more or less attractive or necessary to find expertise, develop expertise, or to change one's view and learn from the other players (Van Assche et al. 2013). Actor/institution configurations and power/knowledge configurations thus also co-evolve and can be understood as the *meta-configuration* marking a certain governance evolution, a *governance path*. In systems terms, one can say that the meta-configuration represents the unique *autopoiesis*, or mode of self-reproduction of governance in a certain community.

9.2 Dependencies and Path Creation

Each path, and the *sites* it connects, is unique. It is marked by different *techniques* of governance. These techniques will be *discursive techniques*, because the building materials for everything in governance are discursive by nature. Each path is marked by *dependencies*, meaning that from point A in the governance path, not every other point is as easy to reach. The structures produced in the reproduction of governance are the results of its autopoiesis and at the same time the preconditions for that reproduction. They restrict the options at each point. We distinguished path dependence, interdependence and goal dependence (Shtaltovna et al. 2013; Van Assche et al. 2011a). Path dependence is the generic name to designate the legacies from the past that influence the current reproduction. Interdependence can be understood as the restrictions in choice that stem from the web of relations that resulted from governance histories. It can refer to the web linking actors and institutions and to the web linking the governance arrangement observed and larger social contexts, including the actors and institutions there. Goal dependence is the influence exerted by constructed futures. This does not only include plans and policies, but any form of shared future envisioned in the governance process. The interplay between these three dependencies creates rigidities in the governance path. It also generates contingency, unanticipated effects that introduce flexibility. *Path creation*, of such flexibility, can also have other sources, among them spaces of freedom that were envisioned in governance design. Each path in other words has its own balance of flexibility and rigidity, dependency and path creation. It is possible that actors are aware of the dependencies typical for their path, but more likely, this insight is very incomplete. The discourse on the identity of actors, territory and on the identity of the governance path, despite being different from what can be seen by outside observers, can have real effects. It can be a productive fiction, and that productivity can include reality effects. We speak of *performativity* when referring to the reality effects of discourse.

9.3 Governance Paths, Objects and Subjects

Governance paths are histories of confrontations between discourses, confrontations of different versions of the world. They are also histories of steering attempts: the development of collectively binding decisions, under the form of policies, laws and plans, that are expected to be collectively binding. These decisions incorporate an understanding of the future, of present and past, upon which expectations about the implementation path of these decisions and about the possibility to steer society by means of these decisions are based. Usually, both grasp of the world and steering power are overestimated. One reason being that social systems are never transparent to each other. This applies to the function system of politics, under which governance falls, and to organizations, a category that applies to most actors (Seidl 2005). Despite this incomplete grasp and control, policy has many real effects, and it can create realities unwittingly, giving the impression that they are caused by the governance decision. Such performative effects of governance can have many sources: it is possible that the policy relies on existing informal coordination mechanisms that already point in the same direction, or that basic concepts, values and goals embedded in the plan are prevalent in society at large, making it easier for situations to emerge that resemble the intentions of policies and plans. It is also possible that the policy, its implementation, its success is presented and measured in such a way that citizens believe it works and start to act accordingly, after which it works. Other paths of performativity are possible. The quality of *performance* of success is relevant, since it can affect the performativity of the policy. Under performance we understand the manner in which the narrative is brought to life in rhetorical enactment. Performance can make a narrative more or less persuasive. If people believe in the narrative, helped by the performance, they can act according to this new reality, and make it real also for external observers.

If we mention performativity, we touch the micro-mechanisms of governance, the discursive mechanisms that accompany the co-evolution of discourses that is typical for governance. Most of these mechanisms also exist outside the realm of governance, some of them acquire a special function within governance, or a unique intensity. We analysed all too briefly some essential discursive mechanisms that are common in governance situations and essential to their understanding. First of all, governance operates with *objects and subjects*. Subjects are social identities as defined in governance, including the identity of the actors present, while objects refer to the other elements of the conceptual worlds narrated in governance (Duineveld and Van Assche 2011; Duineveld et al. 2013; Van Assche et al. 2011a). We discussed techniques of object formation and stabilization, and remarked that no object is entirely stable in the social world, and especially not in governance, where it is subjected to transformative pressures all the time. Objects and subjects are part of discourse, which might fit narrative structures, which can be embedded in broadly distributed ideologies. *Every discursive element and structure* can and will be transformed in governance evolutions, either by social learning and cooperation, or by competition and distinction. Studying in details the processes of *boundary formation* helps in understanding the continuous discursive transformation taking place in governance, the instability of objects, subjects and narratives, as well as the construction of spatial and temporal boundaries governance deploys to structure itself. Also these boundaries, as any other discursive boundary, can be crossed however, enabling the transformation of both sides. Material boundaries can structure discursive boundaries, but one can never be sure how that happens; for that reason we spoke of *empirical boundaries*.

For the understanding of discursive transformation in governance, a few special concepts are particularly useful: *metaphors, open concepts*, and *master signifiers*. All three enable specific forms of boundary-crossing, hence of transformation. All three thrive in the hectic environment of governance, a conceptual pressure-cooker in which new arguments need to be found, new stories invented, new positions taken, critiques made up, distinctions imagined, problems and qualities delineated, and other actors understood and persuaded. Inventiveness is required, just as narrative flexibility and flexible persuasion. Metaphors allow for jumps between conceptual domains and for new simplifications that shed a fresh light on an issue from a new angle. The introduction of metaphors can reorganize the embedding narrative, it can affect other narratives, and change object and subject boundaries. Open concepts create open spaces that ease negotiation between world-views. They create a vague middle ground that can be strategically used when understood as vague, but also used to create a new substantive middle ground, a common understanding or appearance of common understanding. As such, they can, just as metaphors, serve to get out of an impasse, a deadlock, in governance. Master signifiers, then, bring unity to ideological narratives or allow actors to see the ideology in the detail. They can be helpful in keeping actors or coalitions cohesive, but they can also derail governance by producing extreme polarization and politicizing every detail. Master signifiers can be productive fictions that keep a community going, that motivate it to strive for cohesion and to embrace ideals. They can also destroy the middle ground that is needed to keep daily negotiations going.

In the interplay between the various discursive objects and subjects, between actor/institution and power/knowledge configurations, governance reproduces and transforms itself. Paths develop. The analysis of discursive mechanics and transformation is the analysis of power/knowledge at the micro level, where the knowledge (discursive) side is more easily observed. Knowledge of the path as such is needed, of actors and institutions, to sharpen the focus on the power side at the micro level. The same discursive analysis can serve to deepen the understanding of the transformation of actors (subjects) as a result of confrontation with other actors (subjects) and their ideas (objects, narratives), as well as the persuasive effects of the other's views, their strategic assets and their strategies in pursuing their world view (aspects of power). That same analysis can also serve to grasp how actor/institution dialectics are influenced by discursive change (beyond the strategizing according to the rules).

9.4 Methodological Implications

If we consider actor/institution dialectics and power/knowledge dialectics as the two key processes driving the reproduction of governance and the creation of paths, then the partial visibility of these processes might be presented as a problem. We believe however, that a variety of observations in various disciplines necessitates us to adopt the meta-configuration as the ground structure of EGT. It brings cohesion in a hitherto scattered field, and allows us to elaborate a cohesive theory that makes further theoretical development and empirical analysis possible. Methodologically, we believe the partial opacity of the grounding process can be remedied in three ways.

First of all by the mapping of governance paths and their contexts. This implies analysing which actors or subject are involved and how their roles are defined. It also includes analysing the formal and informal coordination mechanisms, the results, and what one can say about implementation. One can look at which forms of expertise are involved and how power relations do play out and alter. Attention should also be given to the broader contexts affected by and affecting the actors and possibly the governance arena itself. This analysis could be facilitated by distinguishing, embedded narratives, embedding ideologies, and embedded scales.

Secondly, a detailed investigation of the discursive mechanics that can be observed in the path (Foucault 1998). The micro-analysis of discursive transformation can serve on the one hand to fill in missing pieces in the reconstruction of the path, while in the other direction; insights gained in path mapping can enhance the understanding of the power side in power/knowledge dialectics. If context mapping took place, discursive analysis can include discursive migration, boundary crossing and its repercussions.

Thirdly, a post hoc categorization of a governance arrangement, in terms of a cohesive set of choice dimensions, can bring yet another perspective to path reconstruction. It can help structuring the path in a series of key choices or positions on key dimensions, choices made on furcating paths in n-dimensional space. If one can observe the responses in other dimensions to changes in one dimension, this can bring further insight in the underlying dynamics of power/knowledge and actor/institution configurations.

Path mapping and path analysis emerge as the key methods to trace the autopoietic identity of a governance arrangement. One can deploy all the concepts presented earlier in this effort. If one is interested in the impact of discursive migration, context mapping will have to be carried out, but the size of the context does not need to be defined a priori. It can follow from the leads discovered in path analysis. Since the underlying configurations cannot easily be observed directly, they have to be reconstructed using path analysis in combination with a finer analysis of discursive transformation. Discursive analysis and analysis of cohesive choice dimensions serve as ways to complete the path analysis *and* the analysis of underlying configurations, in the case of discursive analysis by a micro-study combining induction and deduction, in the case of the dimensional approach by macro analysis based on abduction.

In the practice of research, this approach will necessitate working on several levels at the same time, as the hermeneutic circle does not allow for a clear separation of steps. It will be necessary to jump between scales and between methods and concepts. New insights on one level provide clues —or clear instructions— for the next step on a different level. In these iterations, method, questions, and topic might have to be slightly modified, depending on what one finds. This, we believe, should not be understood as a problem. It only appears as a problem in a theory of science and scientific method that assumes stable entities and predictable processes. For studying autopoietic evolutions, in which literally everything is subjected to transformation by co-evolution and in which the self-understanding of actors and the official understanding of coordinative rules cannot be taken at face value, one simply cannot predict what will emerge in analysis as prior key choices, as key mechanisms, as transparent and opaque areas, as silently influential metaphor or invisible limit to self-transformation.

There is no need to fear however, that the only option remaining is exhaustive mapping, the production of a macro-encyclopedia of micro-governance. Once a preliminary mapping has been carried out, with the topic of investigation in mind, the patterns observed can guide and delineate further investigation, in terms of suitable topics and sub-topics, compatible methods, useful combinations of concepts. A focus on self-transformation will bring different simplifications in the analysis than a focus on the linkage between choice dimensions, or on the influence of a new metaphor, or the reverberations of a particularly traumatic episode, remembered in dramatic narratives. In the next chapter, we will briefly illustrate possible fields of application of EGT.

References

Duineveld, M., & Van Assche, K. (2011). The power of tulips: Constructing nature and heritage in a contested landscape. *Journal of Environmental Policy & Planning, 13*(2), 1–20.

Duineveld, M., Van Assche, K., & Beunen, R. (2013). Making things irreversible. Object stabilization in urban planning and design. *Geoforum, 46*, 16–24.

Foucault, M. (1979). *Discipline and punish: The birth of the prison*. Harmondsworth: Penguin Books.

Foucault, M. (1994). Truth and power. In P. Rabinow (Ed.), *Power. Essential works of Foucault 1954–1984* (Vol. 3).

Foucault, M. (1998). *The will to knowledge. The history of sexuality.* (Vol. 1). London: Penguin Books.

Hacking, I. (1999). Making up people. In M. Biagioli (Ed.), *The science studies reader* (Vol. XVIII, p. 590). New York, NY: Routledge.

North, D. C. (1990). *Institutions, institutional change and economic performance*. Cambridge: Cambridge University Press.

North, D. C. (2005). *Understanding the process of economic change*. Princeton: Princeton University Press.

Seidl, D. (2005). *Organizational identity and self-transformation. An autopoietic perspective*. Aldershot: Ashgate.

Shtaltovna, A., Van Assche, K., & Hornidge, A. K. (2013). Where did this debt come from? Organizational change, role ambiguity and development in rural Khorezm, Uzbekistan. *International Quarterly for Asian Studies. Internationales Asienforum 43*(3–4), 179–197.

Van Assche, K., Beunen, R., & Duineveld, M. (2012). Formal/informal dialectics and the self-transformation of spatial planning systems: An exploration. *Administration & Society* (Online First).

Van Assche, K., Beunen, R., Holm, J., & Lo, M. (2013). Social learning and innovation. Ice fishing communities on Lake Milles Lacs. *Land Use Policy, 34*, 233–242.

Van Assche, K., Beunen, R., Jacobs, J., & Teampau, P. (2011a). Crossing trails in the marshes: Rigidity and flexibility in the governance of the Danube Delta. *Journal of Environmental Planning and Management, 54*(8), 997–1018.

Van Assche, K., Duineveld, M., Beunen, R., & Teampau, P. (2011b). Delineating locals: Transformations of knowledge/power and the governance of the Danube Delta. *Journal of Environmental Policy & Planning, 13*(1), 1–21.

Chapter 10
Policy Formulation and EGT: Making Governance Work

Abstract In this chapter we briefly outline a number of domains of application for EGT, some preliminary insights in each domain, and methodological considerations. We conclude with a reflection on the value of EGT in mapping out the middle ground between libertarian and socialist ideologies.

The prime domain of application of EGT is the analysis of governance as evolving governance. This might sound trivial, but we mention it again because in much of the academic literature on governance, the lack of an evolutionary perspective leads to a series of entwined problems. We mention it explicitly because in neighbouring literatures, too often problems are analysed in technical terms and then dumped in the black box of governance, where the scientific results are supposed to lead to implementation (Beunen 2010). In other words, problems are not always recognized as governance problems, while they should (Fischer 1990). Thus, the non-recognition of problems as governance problems and the non-recognition of governance problems as evolutionary, led to the production of a variety of smokescreens of pretending social utility and societal relevance, behind which scientists can do their work. It led to precepts that are doomed to fail, to a bewildering amount of pointless modelling exercises and decision-support systems (Smith and Stirling 2010; Voß and Bornemann 2011). Moreover it led to public and political disappointment with science as a bringer of collective goods (Beunen and Opdam 2011; McNie 2007; Nowotny et al. 2001). EGT makes things less predictable, yet can help in rendering more transparent what can be made transparent, while pointing at uncertainty and opacity in a precise manner (cf. Fuchs 2001; Luhmann 1989).

The general mixing up of wish and reality that has plagued many studies of governance led to an unfortunate politicization of a set of disciplines and to a specific confusion of wish and reality (Duineveld et al. 2009; Van Assche and Verschraegen 2008). This presented an additional obstacle for constructing and using evolutionary perspectives: the perceived need for single models of governance. For some, the need for conceptual clarity drove the building of transparent

K. Van Assche et al., *Evolutionary Governance Theory*, SpringerBriefs in Economics,
DOI: 10.1007/978-3-319-00984-1_10,

and stable models of governance, models that were detailed enough to be immediately recognizable in reality and structured enough to be amenable to (statistic) analysis. For others, the need to contribute something to society was a reason to build ideal models and criticize existing governance arrangements for not living up to the standards set by the model.

We do acknowledge that each society and each community has narratives and concepts on the ideal society and community, and that these are interwoven with theoretical constructs. How and why they are interwoven, is a process that requires analysis. The presence of 'ideal models' cannot lead to the conclusion that there is such thing as a singular ideal model of governance. The circulating narratives and concepts cannot be used as theoretical models in governance analysis. They ought to be considered self-ascriptions of communities, and/or aspirations that might introduce goal dependencies in the governance path. The five models of democracy we distinguished earlier, for example, ought not to be used as final categorizations, as essences or anchor points of analysis, but as contingent recombinations of discursive elements that acquired longevity in western history since the renaissance. They are useless for analysing the middle ages, useless in many developing countries, and also in a current western community they cannot be used to grasp all complexity of governance. They represent one layer of structure, not the unicity of a governance path. It is precisely that unique pattern of self-transformation of governance, the identity of its autopoiesis, what gives insight in *transformation options*. These transformation options are what many disciplines are interested in. Solving many social problems, or creating new qualities implies in many cases changing governance. Sometimes, scientific observers are aware of this, sometimes not. If they are aware of it, the proposed solutions are often inspired by ideology rather than science.

10.1 Formal Institutions and Citizen Participation

Changes in governance are presented with a high frequency. Regularly one can read that new laws are needed to solve problem a or b, or better politicians, or direct participation by citizens, or a better plan, or more plans. In each case, it might be true or untrue, but very often, authors, schools, and whole disciplines have standard assumptions regarding transformation of governance and society. This presents a problem, since the transformation options are always a result of specific governance evolutions, of the interplay between path dependence, goal dependence and interdependence, and the various discursive mechanisms described. These options should be studied, not be assumed.

EGT is therefore eminently useful in understanding the effects of laws, policies, plans, as formal institutions. After a study of these effects in a community, the insight in newly introduced formalities can be gaged more precisely. As said, comprehensive path mapping is usually not necessary and in applied research it is usually not possible. But especially when application of insights and real-world influence is expected, it is useful at least to take a look at the effects of previous formalities. For that, one cannot rely entirely on existing policy documents or assessments (think performing success, think power/knowledge), neither on existing scientific reports (think scientific identity politics, constraining latent assumptions) nor the portrayals by locals (think problems of self-observation and narrative extrication). A wide variety of sources will be useful, as well as conversations with a wide variety of players, including ones that do not have much at stake (anymore). As far as possible, personal observation should complement the written sources.

Along the same lines, one can argue that EGT is useful for analysing existing forms of citizen participation in governance as well as proposals and the potential for new forms. If citizen participation is formalized, or will be formalized, we refer back to the need for an analysis of other, older, formal institutions. The step of formalization itself can be studied, against the background of a governance path where similar steps might have been taken. It is e.g. possible that the new formality can reinforce less desirable informal coordination forms or power/knowledge configurations (think marginalization, corruption, exploitation) and it is possible that the step towards formality is likely to destabilize local governance, e.g. by introducing new uncertainty (Domingo and Beunen 2013). Indeed, in some context, formalization can increase rather than reduce uncertainty, and thus make transactions more difficult. If the main argument for more citizen participation is 'local knowledge', one can analyse first of all what is meant by that in the specific context and what is expected from it. Secondly one can analyse which forms of knowledge, local or otherwise, played a role in local governance, and what the accepted channels for introducing and playing out new forms of knowledge or expertise are. It is certainly possible that the current situation reveals an undue influence of a few expert groups keeping an elite in place with de-politicizing scientific arguments. It is just as possible that introducing new forms of local knowledge has similarly marginalizing effects.

The effects of formal institutions and of participation forms become more understandable in the context of an evolution, marked by dependencies and embodied in specific patterns of discursive dynamics, of configurations of actors/institutions and power/knowledge. One cannot rely on a standard formula or instrument for enhanced democracy or for solving social problems. Even if one omits most of the conceptual frame of EGT and only studies formal/informal dialectics, this becomes clear. Another immediate implication is that policy transfer and copying of best practices is unlikely to work, unless these policies and practices are tailor-made, in a way that is informed by understanding of the governance path in the receiving community.

10.2 Social Engineering

EGT is useful in exposing social engineering ambitions, in revealing what the limits of steering can be (Van Assche and Verschraegen 2008). Simultaneously it can show what effects policies, laws and plans could have in society, including their steering effects. EGT illustrates that steering powers are structurally overestimated by governmental and other organizations. The forms of steering that might work are, again, dependent on the properties of the governance path. If people are used to being planned or used to follow the law, this can constitute a simple informality that makes steering more realistic, that will give more effects to laws and plans. If social engineering takes place in a very centralized society and is led by the ruling elite, it will probably have effects. If on the other hand, localism, individualism and legalism dominate the governance path, it is unlikely that a plan does much outside the planner's office.

The performance of social engineering has a variety of performative effects. This can be studied, not necessarily to expose steering as fiction, but also to discern steering options that might work and that might be desirable. If a community agrees with the idea of strong central planning, the scientific observer should accept that as well. Especially in such case, it might be useful to show and understand which aspects of steering worked well, what the results where. It might also be useful for EGT to figure out *when* the steering worked best. If we understand every element of governance as changing, then strong steering ambitions might work at one point in time, but not later, or in fewer areas of policy. In the other direction, EGT can study cases of professed decentralization and democatization, of supposedly reduced steering and increased reliance on self-organization, where de facto steering is just as substantial, but under a different name, in a different configuration of actors, initiated from a different level of governance.

EGT can study the rhetorics of regimes fully embracing social engineering and reinventing over and over again after every disappointment, and of regimes totally rejecting any government intervention as socialist and despicable. A study of the discursive mechanics, the causes and effects of these ideologies, and the transformation options in each case can be interesting theoretically, but also practically. It can help to see the effects of polarizing histories of coordination on power/knowledge configurations and on the possibilities to grasp (versions of) the middle ground, and to articulate and implement policies assuming such middle ground.

10.3 Sustainability and Innovation

The potential and limits of environmental policy and planning, e.g. towards sustainability and adaptive governance is another rich terrain for EGT. The recognition of environmental problems introduced new steering ambitions and attempts to integrate various sorts of policies in environmental visions in many societies. The master signifier of sustainability encapsulated not only the impossible ideal of utter harmony with the ecological environment and eternal life for mankind, but also the impossible ideal of full policy integration targeting one goal (Gunder 2006). EGT can serve to analyse what happened discursively and institutionally when green narratives started to permeate society and governance (Latour 2004). It can analyse the effects on actor/institution and power/knowledge configurations, and the effects in society at large. It can study discursive migration, boundary crossing and boundary formation processes accompanying the evolution and distribution of green narratives outside and inside governance, and the implications for the governance path. In addition, it can analyse which options might still be open to reduce unwanted side effects of green rhetoric and practice, and optimize the desirable effects.

The discourse on adaptive governance (towards sustainability) can be considered a more sophisticated version of sustainability thinking, but also this approach can be served with a side dish of EGT (Brunner 2005; Brunner and Lynch 2010; Armitage 2010). While the ideas of adaptation to changing environments and learning from the results of previous policies and policy experiments elsewhere is certainly valuable, there are still issues with which EGT can help. Adaptive governance assumes an observation of external and internal environments that is clear and simple. Moreover, it requires a clear understanding of what worked in the past and elsewhere, and what did not work so well. While this might be easy enough for problems with one or two parameters, when dealing with environmental policies, problems and effects on many other policies and practices, one can expect not only technical difficulties, but more importantly, structural reasons for the performance of success or failure. The approach gives much power to green discourses, so the effect on power/knowledge configurations will be profound, and many things will now be couched in green rhetoric. New differences between public and private self-descriptions of actors will be introduced, new differences between formal and informal institutions. None of this needs to be dramatic or jeopardize the whole idea of adaptive governance, but EGT inspired analyses can warn for harmful fictions of full transparency and fictions of simple steering. Reflexivity is essential to grasp which external environments are constructed internally as a starting point for cycles of adaptation, which issues and parameters are singled, what the narrative conceptualization of the relations between these objects is, how performance and performativity entwine. 'Adaptation' then becomes adaptation also to continuously shifting internal environments of governance.

A similar line of reasoning can be followed regarding 'innovation' (Kooij et al. 2013; Van Assche et al. 2012, 2013). Many countries try to stimulate innovation under the assumptions that there is a lack of innovation, that innovation is the key to economic growth, and that innovation can be stimulated by means of policy. Entrepreneurial scientists see funding possibilities and make various false promises, offering recipes for innovative regions, innovation clusters, innovation parks, creative cities, transition catalysts and so forth (Duineveld et al. 2009). Science and technology studies, actor network theory and the sociology and anthropology of science have shown many times that things do not work like that, that scientific innovation cannot be forced, that it requires autonomy, experiment and long-time horizons, and that scientific and economic innovation are not the same thing. Yet, the social engineering ambitions regarding innovation recur over and over again. EGT can help elucidating the discursive dynamics and power/knowledge configurations behind this, and offer advice on how to extricate oneself from the web of false promises and the self-reinforcing network of smokescreen-producers. At that point, new analyses become possible of innovation and innovation potential; new forms of expertise might be integrated in governance, making it easier to observe the external environment of scientific and economic innovation anew, without immediate cries that something needs to be done, now, by government, following recipe X.

EGT can help in understanding the potential and limits of innovation policy, as in pushing for scientific innovation, demanding this to have economic effects, and forcing a combined role of politics and science in the whole process. Beyond the limits to political steering discussed earlier, we have to add for this topic that the function systems science and economy are opaque for each other, implying among other things that they cannot predict what the next innovation will be in the other function system, nor assess what is really innovative among the new knowledge and new practices in the other system. The economy system cannot assess what the scientific implications of economic changes will be, and neither can science predict the economic consequences of a specific scientific innovation. In addition, even within each function system, it is usually only post factum visible what was innovative, after an idea spurred many other idea. EGT can start from these systems theoretical insights to analyse governance arrangements in their attempts to steer and couple science and economy. Path analyses can reveal de-politicizing effects of innovation policy and the disruptions it can cause in both markets and governance, while delineating spaces for a new reflexivity on innovation. Micro and macro analyses, path mapping and context mapping ought to be combined for that purpose.

10.4 The Autonomy and Rationality of Markets

In the perspective of EGT, markets are autonomous and rational, in the sense that the function system of economy operates under its own logic based on the distinction profit/loss, that it has boundaries and is operationally closed (Luhmann 1988). This is a different understanding of autonomy and rationality than one can find in neo-classical economics and in libertarian philosophies often associated with it. For EGT, markets are autonomous in the sense explained, but at the same time shaped in and by internal evolution and co-evolution with the other function systems and with the organizations and institutions that are conducting and enabling economic transactions (cf. North 2005; Eichholz et al. 2013). Markets for EGT are not the product of governance and not entirely their own product. They are not more rational or efficient when left alone, but develop their own rationality, their own structures and elements in a co-evolution with governance. Because people and organizations participate in economic communication and because the economy is still part of society, the market is sensitive to discursive dynamics that affects governance as well. Boundary crossing can occur and object formation can bear similarities in governance and the markets it tries to regulate. What looks desirable to voters or actors in participatory governance can look desirable to consumers too. Images and narratives of the good life that are exploited and partly produced in the economy, have effects in governance, and these effects can be altered after further discursive transformation in governance and continued discursive migration in and out of governance. Discursive dynamics and social organization create the values that markets calculate and move around.

EGT can be used to study the development of different markets in their co-evolution with unique governance paths. It can reveal the desired and actual results of economic steering attempts, the variety in market forms in their linkage with governance and the embedding of both in societies that are changing themselves. It can look for similarities in formal/informal dialectics in a specific market evolution and a specific governance path. EGT can provide insight in the history of mutual influence of markets and governance in a co-evolution: market players influencing rule making and rules shaping markets. Power/knowledge dialectics in society at large can affect the sharing and not-sharing of institutions by market and governance, and the responses of markets to governance.

Analyses of this sort, inspired by EGT or fully within the frame of EGT, can improve the understanding of the position of markets in society. Understanding the variety of markets and the diversity of evolutionary mechanisms affecting that variety, can help actors in governance to see that there is a middle road between neo-classical economics and its free market idea and social engineering models. In fact, it shows that there are many roads in between, and that some are more feasible than others starting from the current position in unique governance paths and market evolutions. Grasping the uniqueness of these paths appears once again as essential.

10.5 Development

For EGT, every community and society is in development (cf. Greif 2006; Mosse 2005). Development cannot be understood as one final state, or a process that is similar for all societies. Development is visible in a path of governance and a market evolution. Interventions aiming at 'development' (as discursive construct) ought to take into account these evolutions and the transformation options they reveal. Similarities between paths are possible of course, and one source is the similarity between goal dependencies that can be introduced by means of policy and planning. Introducing the same goals and policies in different paths will however produce mostly different outcomes and can just as well contribute to a divergence than to a convergence of paths.

If policy import for development purposes is considered, EGT would draw the attention to fit with informal institutions and power/knowledge configuration. It would, in addition, point at the importance of timing: EGT in this respect is a theory of windows of opportunities. These windows are not always visible for outside observers and it is not always opportune to reveal their existence and to make them transparent before the deal is done.

We agree with William Easterly and his distinction between searchers and planners (Easterly 2006). If one decides to see 'development' as an overarching goal of governance, despite all the problems associated with overarching goals, and if one decides to import policies from somewhere else for that purpose, despite the sorry track record of this approach, then at least one should be extremely cautious with grand strategy and comprehensive planning. Only under rare conditions this might work-indeed, China, and only after a complete reorganization of society in early communism laid the groundwork for economic planning. As a general maxim, it seems wise follow the searchers, to cultivate reflexivity, awareness of the reproductive modes of governance and its underlying configurations, and to embrace institutional experimentalism. It is important to foster local experiment with different market and governance forms, and see whether certain policy imports, after their reinterpretation and modification in local configurations, have desirable effects.

References

Armitage, D. R. (2010). *Adaptive capacity and environmental governance*. London: Springer.

Beunen, R. (2010). *The governance of nature: How nature conservation ambitions have been dashed in planning practices*. Wageningen: Wageningen University.

Beunen, R., & Opdam, P. (2011). When landscape planning becomes landscape governance, what happens to the science? *Landscape and Urban Planning, 100*(4), 324–326.

Brunner, R. D. (2005). *Adaptive governance: Integrating science, policy, and decision making*. New York: Columbia University Press.

Brunner, R. D., & Lynch, A. H. (2010). *Adaptive governance and climate change*. Boston: American Meteorological Society.

Domingo, I., & Beunen, R. (2013). Regional planning in the Catalan Pyrenees: Strategies to deal with actors' expectations, perceived uncertainties and conflicts. *European Planning Studies, 21*(2), 187–203.

Duineveld, M., Beunen, R., Van Assche, K., During, R., & van Ark, R. (2009). The relationship between description and prescription in transition research. In K. J. Poppe, C. Termeer & M. Slingerland (Eds.), *Transitions towards sustainable agriculture and food chains in peri-urban areas* (pp. 392). Wageningen: Wageningen Academic Publishers.

Easterly, W. (2006). *The white man's burden: Why the West's efforts to aid the rest have done so much ill and so little good*. Oxford: Oxford University Press.

Eichholz, M., Van Assche, K., Oberkircher, L., & Hornidge, A. K. (2013). Trading capitals? Bourdieu, land and water in rural Uzbekistan. *Journal of Environmental Planning and Management, 56*(6), 868–892.

Fischer, F. (1990). *Technocracy and the politics of expertise*. Newbury Park: Sage Publications.

Fuchs, S. (2001). *Against essentialism: A theory of culture and society*. Cambridge: Harvard University Press.

Greif, A. (2006). *Institutions and the path to the modern economy: Lessons from medieval trade*. Cambridge: Cambridge University Press.

Gunder, M. (2006). Sustainability. Planning's saving grace or road to perdition? *Journal of Planning Education and Research, 26*(2), 208–221.

Kooij, H., Van Assche, K., & Lagendijk, A. (2013). Open concepts as crystallization points and enablers of discursive configurations: the case of the innovation campus in the Netherlands. *European Planning Studies* (Online First).

Latour, B. (2004). *Politics of nature. How to bring the sciences into democracy*. Cambridge: Harvard University Press.

Luhmann, N. (1988). *Die Wirtschaft der Gesellschaft*. Frankfurt am Main: Suhrkamp.

Luhmann, N. (1989). *Ecological communication*. Chicago: University of Chicago Press.

McNie, E. C. (2007). Reconciling the supply of scientific information with user demands: an analysis of the problem and review of the literature. *Environmental Science & Policy, 10*(1), 17–38.

Mosse, D. (2005). *Cultivating development: An ethnography of aid policy and practice*. London: Pluto Press.

North, D. C. (2005). *Understanding the process of economic change*. Princeton: Princeton University Press.

Nowotny, H., Scott, P., & Gibbons, M. (2001). *Re-thinking science: Knowledge and the public in an age of uncertainty*. Cambridge, UK: Polity.

Smith, A., & Stirling, A. (2010). The politics of social-ecological resilience and sustainable socio-technical transitions. *Ecology and Society, 15*(1), 11.

Van Assche, K., Beunen, R., Holm, J., & Lo, M. (2013). Social learning and innovation. Ice fishing communities on Lake Milles Lacs. *Land Use Policy, 34*, 233–242.

Van Assche, K., Salukvadze, J., & Duineveld, M. (2012). Under pressure: Speed, vitality and innovation in the reinvention of Georgian planning. *European Planning Studies, 20*(6), 999–1015.

Van Assche, K., & Verschraegen, G. (2008). The limits of planning: Niklas Luhmann's systems theory and the analysis of planning and planning ambitions. *Planning Theory, 7*(3), 263–283.

Voß, J. P., & Bornemann, B. (2011). The politics of reflexive governance: Challenges for designing adaptive management and transition management. *Ecology and Society, 16*, 9.

MIX
Papier aus verantwortungsvollen Quellen
Paper from responsible sources
FSC® C105338

If you have any concerns about our products,
you can contact us on
ProductSafety@springernature.com

In case Publisher is established outside the EU,
the EU authorized representative is:
Springer Nature Customer Service Center GmbH
Europaplatz 3, 69115 Heidelberg, Germany

Printed by Libri Plureos GmbH
in Hamburg, Germany